BIZARRE SCOTLAND

David Long

Constable • London

CONSTABLE

First published in Great Britain in 2014 by Constable

Text copyright @ David Long, 2014
Illustrations copyright @ Sara Mulvanny, 2014

The moral right of the author has been asserted.

A CIP catalogue record for this book
is available from the British Library.

ISBN 978-1-47211-746-5 (hardback)
ISBN 978-1-47211-747-2 (ebook)

Typeset in Stempel Garamond by
Initial Typesetting Services, Edinburgh
Printed and bound by CPI Group (UK) Ltd, Croydon, CR0 4YY

Constable is an imprint of
Constable & Robinson Ltd
100 Victoria Embankment
London EC4Y 0DY

An Hachette UK Company
www.hachette.co.uk

www.constablerobinson.com

Contents

	Introduction	v
1.	Royal Scotland	1
2.	Natural Scotland	11
3.	Tourist Scotland	24
4.	Transport Scotland	34
5.	Sporting Scotland	48
6.	Secret Scotland	60
7.	Island Scotland	73
8.	Inventing Scotland	85
9.	Aristocratic Scotland	97
10.	Building Scotland	112
11.	Eccentric Scotland	124
12.	Ceremonial Scotland	137
13.	Fighting Scotland	148
14.	Ghostly Scotland	160
15.	Witch-crazed Scotland	172
16.	Criminal Scotland	182
17.	Gruesome Scotland	192
18.	Screening Scotland	201
19.	Consuming Scotland	212

Introduction

With its battle-scarred past, a long and romantic history, and the incomparable majesty of its wild peaks and mysterious lochs, Scotland has as great a claim on the traveller's imagination as anywhere in the world.

The Scots know it, too, and beyond its natural glories will proudly tell of their countrymen who invented Tarmac, the telephone and television. They'll tell visitors how it was a Scot who discovered penicillin, a Scot who came up with the idea for the Bank of England, and a Scot who established the BBC as the institution it is today.

But even they know only half the story. How many remember the Scottish factory where cars used to be built 'by ladies for ladies', for example, or knew that punters enjoying the show at Glasgow's Britannia Panopticon – Britain's oldest surviving music hall – used to keep warm by filling their pockets with horse dung, which, once cold, would be hurled at performers who failed to please?

Do they know about the Edinburgh car dealer's son who first drove a car to the top of Ben Nevis back in 1911? Why a Clydeside shipbuilder built a yacht shaped like a fish for a Russian Tsarina who didn't like boats? Or why once a year the queen likes to pull on a pair of rubber gloves during her stay at Balmoral, and why the Scottish football team used to dress in pink and primrose?

The truth is, it's not just the lochs that are mysterious in Scotland. If you've ever wondered what the 17th-century Scottish linguist meant when he spoke about 'anfractuosities' and 'cathetobasall', or how much the newly crowned Edward VII enjoyed smashing to pieces his mother's collection of china statues of John Brown, or why the Duke of Hamilton had his feet cut off, then this book is for you.

In it you'll find the answers to questions even the Scots themselves don't ask. Which Scottish city council has a stated policy to extend a 'warm and peaceful' welcome to visitors from outer space. The location of the world's oldest indoor loo. Or how much it costs to strangle and burn a witch. It's all here, from the country's ugliest building to its oddest jobs, from the most unsavoury-sounding wig to the most famous village that never existed. *Bizarre Scotland* celebrates the great country like never before – and it's all true.

David Long, October 2014

I

Royal Scotland

'I feel a sort of reverence in going over these scenes in this most beautiful country, which I am proud to call my own, where there was such devoted loyalty to the family of my ancestors – for Stuart blood is in my veins . . .'

Queen Victoria's journal entry in 1873

For years the royal family's most vociferous opponent was a Scot, the staunch republican and MP for Fife Willie Hamilton (1917–2000). But in spite of this, thanks to Balmoral, Gordonstoun and a love of reeling, Britain's first family has long had strong links north of the border, and the Scots seem on the whole to love having them come to stay.

When in Scotland

Travelling in Scotland, as heir to the throne, the Prince of Wales is correctly referred to as the Duke of Rothesay or, in Gaelic, Diùc Baile Bhòid. The title refers to a Scottish Act of Parliament that was passed in 1469 but refers quite specifically to 'the first-born

Prince of the King of Scots for ever'. In theory this means that if a Prince of Wales were to die before succeeding to the throne his heir would not be entitled to the same courtesy.

The sovereign has also resorted to a number of aliases when moving through her realm. For a while Queen Victoria called herself the Countess of Balmoral in the mistaken belief that in this way she could travel incognito (the Countess of Lancaster was another favourite disguise) while Edward VII occasionally made a similarly unsuccessful bid to hide behind the moniker 'Charles Renfrew'.

As a pupil at Gordonstoun, Prince Philip once signed his name as the Earl of Baldwin when asked by a tourist for his autograph. His youngest son was also known as Earl during his time at the school – from his initials Edward Anthony Richard Louis – but then nicknamed 'Jaws' when he was fitted with braces for his teeth. Prince Andrew's nickname at the school was 'The Sniggerer', and Prince Charles's 'School Guardian' as he was headboy. (Quite a naughty one, though: in 1963 the newspapers revealed he had been caught in a pub in Stornoway ordering a glass of cherry brandy.)

Maintaining the nicety of treating Scotland as a genuinely separate country, the last of the Hanoverians, King William IV (1765–1837), technically succeeded to four distinct thrones. On the death of his brother, and as the oldest person ever to succeed as a British sovereign, he became William I of Hanover, William II of Ireland, William III of Scotland and William IV of England.

Welcomed into the world at her grandparents' Glamis Castle in 1930, HRH Princess Margaret was the first royal in direct line to the throne to have been born in Scotland for 300 years. She also owes her marriage to a Scot because it was at the 1956 wedding of her friend Colin Tennant, 3rd Baron Glenconner (see Aristocratic Scotland), that she first spotted the official photographer, Anthony Armstrong-Jones, whom subsequently she married.

Dressing the Part

In 1822, on the first royal visit north of the border since the '45 Rebellion, George IV lifted the longstanding ban on the playing of bagpipes and truly entered into the spirit by dressing head to foot in tartan. Unfortunately no one pointed out that he had his kilt on back-to-front. (At the start of the same visit Sir Walter Scott had seized a goblet from which the king had been drinking and vowed it would forever remain in his family, an heirloom to mark this historic occasion. Unfortunately, according to Thackeray, he had 'clapped the precious glass in his pocket [then] sat down on it and broke it when he got home'.)

On a visit to Balmoral some thirty years later Queen Victoria was reportedly not amused to witness the young Lord Claud Hamilton (then aged ten) turning somersaults in his own kilt and in the process demonstrating the traditional Highland habit of wearing nothing underneath.

Funnily enough her ancestor George III had had a similar shock, once shouting when at a levee, 'Keep the ladies at the back, keep them at the back,' when a respectful Scottish colonel's deep bow caused his kilt to ride up. And when William IV wore one on his first visit to Scotland, and expressed concern that it was perhaps a little short, a tactful lady courtier assured him that 'As your Majesty stays so short a time in Scotland the more we see of you the better.'

He might have been fooled, but the queen wouldn't have been: in the 1960s when Princess Anne suggested she try a miniskirt she dismissed the suggestion, saying she was 'not a film star'. Then again, and I know this is hard to imagine, in 1969 she did agree to dress up as a beatnik (for a Come-as-a-Beatnik Ball at Balmoral) and around the same time her brother-in-law Lord Snowdon was spotted in the village of Ballater wearing tweed knickerbockers and a 'brown velvet anorak'.

George VI also went through a tartan phase, ordering not one but two tartan dinner jackets in February 1950. Pictures of him wearing them very rarely come to light, suggesting His Majesty had been stung by the words of the po-faced *Tatler* editor Mr John Taylor, who decided 'not to make any comment. Presumably it is intended for wear in private only.'

Life at Balmoral

- Describing it as her 'pretty castle in the old Scotch style', Queen Victoria purchased the Balmoral estate for her beloved Prince Albert after unexpectedly inheriting around half a million pounds in 1852 from someone she had never met and of whom she had never previously heard.

- The money came from John Camden Neild, an eccentric and slightly reclusive figure who lived on the Thames at Chelsea. Despite being worth perhaps £40 million at current values Neild would routinely hitch rides on carters' wagons rather than pay a coach fare into London, and never cleaned his clothes for fear this would wear them out. He made occasional bequests during his lifetime but frugality was very much his watchword, and on his death he left his entire fortune to his sovereign, 'begging for Her Majesty's most gracious acceptance of the same, for her sole use and benefit, and her heirs, &c'.

- Since then most of those heirs and their families have loved the place as much as she did, but Edward VII was a notable exception and memorably described it as 'the Highland Barn of 1,000 draughts'. He wasn't mad about Sandringham either (calling it 'Dickens in a Cartier setting') but the Queen is very happy at Balmoral, although curiously she is reported to have said that at Sandringham she feels 'a great deal more remote from London than at Balmoral'.

- The 42,000-acre estate is very much a holiday home, and so high jinks are only to be expected. Practical jokes played on visitors to Scotland have included apple pie beds (organised by Diana, Princess of Wales) and everything between guests' sheets from dried peas to dead birds and even a live lobster, which Edward VII was wont to slip in.

- Years later his son George V banned alcohol from Balmoral for the duration of the Great War, although it was well known at the time that when he left the table saying he needed to 'attend to a small matter of business' he was actually sneaking off to his study for a glass of port. The traditional shooting was also largely curtailed during the war years, the only game shot being for the benefit of local farmers, servants and the sick.

- Ordinarily if unusually, His Majesty drank a single malt with his dinner. Princess Margaret did this too, probably because she liked neither white wine nor champagne. Albeit diluted, whisky also forms part of the traditional shooting lunch at Balmoral, where each 'piece' comprises a fairly modest bill of fare of a stuffed roll, an apple and a slice of plum pudding.

- Today when the queen or her family is en route to Balmoral special arrangements are made with National Air Traffic Services (NATS). These ensure that a strip of sky ten miles wide is cleared of all other aircraft on the route from London to Aberdeen. A similar arrangement was made between London and Caithness when the queen mother visited her Castle of Mey. (Arriving by helicopter she once observed that 'the chopper has transformed my life – even more than it transformed Anne Boleyn's'.) Designated Purple Air Ways, these strips must be avoided by all civil and military aircraft for a period of half an hour before members of the royal family are scheduled to travel.

- Grey with red and black overchecks, the sett of the Balmoral tartan was invented by Prince Albert in 1853 and is said to echo the appearance of the rough-hewn granite of Royal Deeside. It is worn by HM Queen and members of the royal family can wear it only with her express permission. Her personal piper is also permitted to wear it but estate workers and ghillies are not, and instead sport the Balmoral tweed.

What They Like Doing at Balmoral . . .

There's a nine-hole golf course on the estate and a cricket pitch, but for a while the Duke of Edinburgh liked nothing more than to dig. The lake at Balmoral was excavated by him personally using a bulldozer on loan from the Army.

Briefly the royal household also used to enjoy American-style toasted triple-decker sandwiches. These had been introduced to Balmoral by Mrs Wallis Simpson during a visit to the castle in 1936.

Favourite television viewing at Balmoral has traditionally included *Dad's Army* and *Brideshead Revisited* (for the queen and the late queen mum); *Fawlty Towers* (Prince Andrew); and *Edward and Mrs Simpson* and David Attenborough's *Life on Earth* (Prince Charles).

The queen is also a big fan of the Beatles' *Yellow Submarine*, and is known to have watched it many times. Performances of the national anthem on television are said to have irritated the queen mother greatly, however. She would always insist the set be switched off immediately, telling those assembled, 'Unless one is there it is embarrassing, like hearing the Lord's Prayer while playing canasta.'

Apparently the queen also likes to wash the dishes at Balmoral, but only once a year, in private, after a family barbecue, with no one else drying or putting away.

. . . And What They Don't Like Doing at Balmoral

At one point during her long reign Queen Victoria ordered 'No Smoking' notices to be posted around the place, to the irritation of several of her guests. In the event only one of these chose to ignore the decree. King Albert of Saxony decided after two days of painful abstinence to light a cigar on the grounds that, as a monarch himself, he was entitled to make up his own rules.

Queen Victoria couldn't bear coal fires and insisted on wood ones, although as often as not she would refuse to have these lit – or even have them put out – when she felt that a particular room was 'quite warm enough'. The music of Handel was also banned, and once the ladies had retired after dinner the gentlemen were rarely allowed more than a few minutes to enjoy their port and manly chatter before rejoining their wives.

George V refused to allow his son, the future Edward VIII, to enter into the spirit of the place, and on hearing him practising with a set of bagpipes advised him not to do it again. 'Leave this art to the Highlanders,' he said. 'They know what they're doing.'

While it is unlikely that many people get away with telling the queen what to do, Queen Elizabeth the Queen Mother once asked her daughter (who had just requested another glass of wine), 'Is that wise? You know you have to reign all afternoon.'

The queen mother also preferred lady guests at Balmoral not to wear trousers and, never wearing them herself, would pull waders on over a skirt when out fly-fishing. Meanwhile her daughter, while happy to be seen out on the grouse moor – of which the royal family owns many thousands of acres around Balmoral, Birkhall and Glen Doll – never eats the birds themselves, nor snails or oysters.

Bad Manners in the Borders

In a rare public gaffe, Queen Mary praised the appearance of a new park she had been asked to open in Glasgow but then complained to a local councillor, 'What a shame about all the houses around it.'

Stalking near Balmoral George V, though a keen shot, missed a relatively easy stag. Clearly irritated, he ordered the stalker to 'take this damned rifle away and never let me see it again'. To his surprise the Scotsman replied, telling the king, 'Your Majesty, don't waste your breath damning the rifle. It was a very bad shot.'

The Scottish politician the 5th Earl of Rosebery was similarly ticked off by Edward VII. After he presented himself at court in a suit rather than dress uniform, the king affected to believe the former prime minister was an American. (George V inherited the same stickiness for correct form and used to insist his children wore white tie and their Garter stars even when the family was dining alone.)

Well known not to suffer fools at all, let alone gladly, as a young showjumper in Ayrshire in 1972 Princess Anne snapped at a television cameraman, 'Don't you think I've got enough problems without you?'

Prince Philip has also put his foot in it occasionally. In the 1960s, whilst speaking to members of the Scottish Women's Institute, he surprised them by declaring, 'You know, British women can't cook. They are very good at decorating food and making it attractive. But they have a complete inability to cook.'

In the 1930s when George V met the novelist John Buchan (aka the 1st Lord Tweedsmuir) he admitted he didn't read a great deal but had very much enjoyed Buchan's popular classic *The Thirty-Nine Steps*. Unfortunately Queen Mary followed this up by telling him that the king didn't have much time for reading at all 'and when he does I'm afraid he reads the most awful rubbish'.

It wasn't unknown for King George to attempt to put guests at their ease, however. When one of them broke wind at dinner one evening he was quick to kick a nearby dog whilst growling at it, 'Filthy brute'. Unfortunately the dog was made of porcelain, and shattered into tiny fragments.

The Affair of John Brown

Queen Victoria showed rather more grace when out walking with her faithful manservant, John Brown. After a few too many Brown stumbled and tripped over. Rather than telling him off for being drunk, Her Majesty ignored the obvious and instead said that she too had felt the ground shake from a presumed earth tremor.

One feels her son might have been rather more censorious. No fan of Brown's, on the death of his mother the new King Edward VII lost no time in smashing all the commemorative statuettes of Brown he could lay his hands on. (He was also presumably instrumental in persuading his mother not to publish a small book she had written, although he was unable to prevent her from printing a number of copies of *The Biography of John Brown* at her own expense.)

More Retail than Regal

Woolworths was never awarded the Royal Warrant for rendering goods or services, but in 1939 the future Queen Elizabeth II, then a teenager, bought all her Christmas presents from a branch of the store in Aberdeen.

Another royal retail connection: in the 1980s Princess Diana's mother, the Hon. Frances Shand Kydd, owned a small newsagent and tobacconist's in the coastal town of Oban. (In fact there are a few of these: Princess Michael's mother had a dress shop in Sydney, Australia, and both Angus Ogilvy and Anthony Armstrong-Jones worked as waiters before marrying their princesses.)

Even more surprisingly, perhaps, in the 1950s the queen mother organised a fête in the grounds of Crathie Church near Balmoral and insisted that various family members – including her daughter – run one of the stalls during the afternoon.

In Closing: What Scotland Means to Them

Queen Victoria called it her 'loved and blessed land' and, as a nod to ancient Scottish superstitions, forbade any of her children from marrying in May for fear it would bring them bad luck.

Queen Alexandra once made the mistake of comparing Scotland unfavourably with Ireland, which she thought 'far more beautiful'. Queen Mary was more sensitive, and seeking a way to describe the stunning scenery of Norway eventually settled on a description of 'a mixture of Scotland and Switzerland'.

One of the Queen's particular favourites is reportedly Scottish country dancing, although in her youth she was also very good at tap and learned to do the Twist. Queen Elizabeth the Queen Mother was also a great fan of the fishing here, and something of an expert. Well into her old age she was still landing twenty-pounders each season at Balmoral.

Of course, she was a Scot herself, and as a girl the young Lady Elizabeth Bowes-Lyon had enjoyed dressing up in the nursery at Glamis Castle. Insisting family members call her 'Princess Elizabeth' even then, and with a dressing-up chest that included genuine Tudor clothes, she soon became known for her sharp wit and shrewdness. Neither was ever better displayed than in a brief cable from London to her father when she ran out of funds: 'SOS,' it read: 'LSD RSVP.'

(Glamis Castle is also the only place where our present sovereign has been known to say anything even remotely controversial about religion. As a young girl staying at with her grandparents Princess Elizabeth was told by a visiting cleric that he would send her a book as a present. To this the future Defender of the Faith told him, 'Not about God. I know all about him already.')

And Finally: A Corner of a Field which is Forever Scotland

Despite their love for the country only two members of the British royal family have been buried in Scotland. Edward VII's granddaughter, HRH Princess Arthur of Connaught, was cremated in 1959 and had her ashes interred at the chapel of Mar Lodge in Braemar together with those of her son, the 2nd Duke of Connaught, who had predeceased her.

2

Natural Scotland

'Your country consists of two things, stone and water. There is, indeed, a little earth above the stone in some places, but a very little; and the stone is always appearing. It is like a man in rags; the naked skin is still peeping out.'

Samuel Johnson, quoted in James Boswell's
Journal of a Tour to the Hebrides

Johnson, of course, was the exception, and it's a sad man who can't appreciate Scotland's beauty and quite outstanding natural heritage. The novelist Elizabeth Smart came closer when she described 'a glorious riot of colour blazing red across the moors and gleaming every shade of gold in the forests of sheltered glens. Those achingly beautiful images would be painted again and again across the hills and in the shivering waters of the mountain tarns.'

Scotland's Top Ten Rare Mammals

- Despite the name **common seals** are much, much rarer than grey ones, with approximately 83,000 examples of *Phoca* *vitulina* living in Europe, compared with around 400,000 *Halichoerus grypus* (an unfortunate name for the poor grey, which translates as 'hook-nosed sea pig'). These days around a third of Europe's Common Seals live in Scottish waters, and it is illegal to harass one without a licence.

- **Sika deer** were introduced to the British Isles from the Orient during the reign of Queen Victoria. Even now it is thought that every living example running wild in Scotland is descended from a single stag and three hinds that were acquired in 1860 by Mervyn Wingfield, 7th Viscount Powerscourt, for his deer park at Enniskerry in Ireland.

- It is illegal to harm or obstruct a **pipistrelle bat**, but one wonders why anyone would risk injuring such a helpful beast. Each one consumes approximately 3,000 of those pesky Highland midges every single night.

- Although the name **badger** is thought to be derived from the French word *bêcheur* (meaning digger), the animal is sufficiently at home here in Scotland for a family group to be known as a clan.

- The sovereign enjoys an ancient right entitling her to claim any **sperm whale** that washes up on the Scottish shore. Even so, when a forty five-foot specimen was found dead at Portobello beach in Edinburgh in January 2014 it was unceremoniously towed away and dumped on a landfill site.

- Scotland's most famous **otter** – the star of Gavin Maxwell's *Ring of Bright Water* – was actually an immigrant. Though raised by the author on 'Camusfeàrna' (in reality one of the Sandaig Islands in the Sound of Sleat), Mijbil was born in the marshes of Iraq. Subsequently identified by staff at London Zoo as a representative of a hitherto unknown species, she was given the Latin name *Lutrogale perspicillata maxwelli*. This hugely annoyed Maxwell's fellow author and erstwhile friend Wilfred Thesiger, who had actually found the beast in the first place. The film of the book was shot mainly around Seil Island in the Firth of Lorne and Argyll.

- **Pine martens**, those cute-looking but ferocious cat-sized members of the weasel family, generally live in woodlands but have been known to move in with human families (usually, thank goodness, preferring the roof space). Adept at catching squirrels on the fly, they are sufficiently sure-footed to chase one at speed through the upper branches of trees.

- That said, the **red squirrel**, Scotland's beleaguered native, has much to thank the pine marten for. Research published in 2013 seems to indicate that the latter kills proportionately more grey squirrels than red ones. Because of this it is thought to be a major factor in the recent revival of the threatened native species in areas such as Pitlochry and Aberfeldy in Perthshire and in the Trossachs.

- Frequently mistaken for rats – Ratty in Kenneth Grahame's *The Wind in the Willows* is actually a **European water vole** – this shy little rodent is a rarity in Scotland despite the female's ability to give birth to a new litter every twenty-two days. Able to swim fifty feet underwater on a single breath, they cleverly kick up mud from the riverbed to provide a squid-like cloud to obscure their precise whereabouts when spotted by a hungry otter.

- The last surviving feline species to be found living in the wild in Britain, the **Scottish wildcat** – aka the Highland Tiger – can hear whilst asleep and has eyesight reckoned to be seven times more acute than a human's. Able to run at 30 mph, and pound for pound as strong as an actual tiger, they make lousy pets even when hand-raised from a kitten.

SCOTLAND'S FIRST METEORITE

. . . Or at least the first one we know about. This fell before lunch on 5 April 1804, landing in a disused quarry at High Possil, a suburb of Glasgow. More than 200 years later it is something of a rarity as only three other meteorites have since been recorded in Scotland.*

According to a report in the *Herald and Advertiser* a little over three weeks later, three men working nearby 'were alarmed with a singular noise, which continued, they say, for about two minutes, seeming to proceed from the south-east to the north-west. At first, it appeared to resemble four reports from the firing of cannon, afterwards, the sound of a bell, or rather of a gong, with a violently whizzing noise; and lastly they heard a sound, as if some hard body struck, with very great force, the surface of the earth.'

A 'misty commotion' having been observed in the atmosphere – a cause of considerable concern in more religious times than our own – it took several days to locate all the fragments that had fallen to earth, and sadly the largest of these was then discarded and is now lost. Others found their way to the Hunterian Museum at the University of Glasgow, enabling the meteorite to be identified as being of a common type – classified as a L6 olivine-hypersthene chondrite – but containing minerals only found very rarely on the Earth.

*Two more fell in Perthshire (1830 and 1917) and a third near Glenrothes on Speyside. The latter was found as recently as 1998 but presumed to have fallen much earlier, as it was heavily weathered. Four is not many, but given that more than 600 square miles of Scotland are made up of freshwater lakes and lochs the chances are that one or two have sunk without trace.

Scotland's Top Ten Rare Birds

- In June 2013 birders from all over the UK travelled to the Western Isles to see a rare example of the **white-throated needletail**. For some reason the bird, which breeds in China and winters in Australasia, had been spotted on Harris. Said to be the fastest bird in the world in level flight, this one was unfortunately killed almost as soon as it arrived after flying into the blades of a supposedly environmentally friendly wind turbine.

- The fear of something similar happening to another uncommon visitor the same year was enough to halt the development of a massive wind farm on Shetland. A thirty-acre site had been earmarked for more than 100 turbines, but the project was canned when a high court judge learned that it was an important breeding ground for the graceful **whimbrel**.

- Once widespread across Britain but killed in vast numbers by fisherman who like to use its feathers for making trout flies, the **dotterel** is now reduced to as few as fifty breeding pairs. In summer this member of the plover family was seen only on Cairngorm mountain tops, the males taking the usual female role of sitting on the eggs and raising the young. It was the bird's singular misfortune to be a great favourite of James VI, who shot them in huge numbers.

- One of the reasons you don't see a **golden eagle** very often is that each breeding pair (they are impressively monogamous) requires a vast territory of 60–70 square miles of largely empty countryside. Also, in a dive they can fly at 150 mph, which is more than enough to outrun someone peering through binoculars or reaching for a cameraphone.

- There are a great many rarities that make landfall on the north-east coast of Scotland or Shetland. Seen in Britain on only three occasions, the **Isabelline wheatear** has made it to Scotland just once, when an example of this Tanzanian relative of the thrush somehow turned up in Aberdeen.

- Clearly numerous during the Iron Age, and a popular dish to set before kings in centuries past, the **common crane** was more or less eaten to extinction during the Middle Ages. Recently the birds have returned to these shores, however, and at the last count there were seventeen breeding pairs in Great Britain. These include one in north-east Scotland, which has produced two chicks, but the RSPB is refusing to say more on the grounds that the birds 'don't like to mix it with humans'.

- Huge, delicious and sedentary – a bad combination for any animal that spends most of its time on the ground (just ask the dodo) – the **capercaillie** became extinct in Britain in 1785. Since being reintroduced several times since 1837 the grouse's fat cousin has unsurprisingly found itself back on the red list for species at risk.

- Another potential victim of green technologies, the **black-throated diver** is so poor at walking that it needs to nest at the water's edge so it can shuffle around on its belly. Until recently this ruled out several lochs used to power hydro-electric schemes in the north-west (where the water's edge moves back and forth as the level fluctuates) but now special floating 'islands' have been created to help out the hapless creatures.

- An example of the splendidly named **Ascension frigatebird**, so-called for its breeding ground on the rocky slopes of Boatswain Bird Island just off Ascension Island in the tropical Atlantic, was found dying on Tiree in 1953. Sixty years later a juvenile of the same species made its way to Bowmore on Islay, but presumably only after being blown off course, as its preferred diet consists of turtles.

- A rare visitor to Shetland and the Cairngorms, the **snowy owl** hasn't bred in Scotland since the 1970s. This may be because even the worst winters here are a bit too warm, the owl's thick plumage and heavily feathered feet being better adapted to life many miles north of the Arctic Circle. An adult will happily consume smaller owls whole and as many as 1,800 lemmings in a year, and is intelligent enough to follow traplines in search of mammals to eat if it can't be bothered to hunt.

Arguably more impressive than any of this lot, however, is 'Lady', Britain's oldest breeding osprey, who in 2014 returned to the Loch of the Lowes reserve near Dunkeld in Perthshire for the twenty-fourth year in succession. Thought to be twenty-nine years old, making her the world's oldest known breeding raptor, at the time of writing she had just laid her 69th egg before flying back to Africa for the winter months, leaving her partner to feed the chicks.

SCOTLAND'S WORST-EVER WEATHER

Although recent experience suggests there is more to come – as when houses in Footdee in Aberdeen were blanketed by a foot-thick creamy-white layer of foam in September 2012 (actually a wind-whipped mixture of sand and water) – Scotland can lay claim to several unenviable UK weather records. These include:

The **coldest temperature ever recorded** in the British Isles was at Altnaharra in Sutherland where the mercury dipped to minus 27.2°C on 30 December 1995.

On 26 June 1953 at Eskdalemuir in Dumfriesshire more than three inches (actually 80 mm) of **rain fell in a single half hour**.

For **rainfall over a 24-hour period** the record goes to Sloy Main Adit (Argyll and Bute), which on 17 January 1974 received a 238-mm soaking, an astonishing nine inches or more.

At Fraserburgh in Aberdeenshire on 13 February 1989 the **highest recorded windspeed** reached 142 mph, but that was only at low level. The **official absolute windspeed record** was recorded higher up on Cairn Gorm above Aviemore. On 20 March 1986 the wind reached an incredible 173 mph.

(Unofficially Shetland beat it with a recorded speed of 177 mph back in 1962, but this could actually be correct as it was recorded by professionals, at RAF Saxa Vord.)

And the good stuff? Well, it does happen. The aforementioned Tiree in Argyll and Bute notched up a **record sunshine total** of 329.1 hours during the course of May 1975, barely fifty hours behind the south coast of the so-called English Riviera.

Stop Press: New Species Always Welcome in Scotland, Says Man

In 2013, in a response to a bizarre Freedom of Information request from a member of the public, Glasgow City Council confirmed that it would welcome contact from extra-terrestrial species, assuring new arrivals of a 'warm and peaceful' reception.

A spokesman for the local authority admitted that there were no specific plans in place to organise such a welcome, saying this was because 'the general consensus ... is that contact is most likely to be made through radio communication, since faster-than-light travel remains in the realms of fiction and it would take an improbably long time to travel between the stars at sub-light speed. As the council does not own or control any radio telescopes we do not expect to pick up any signals from space.'

He was keen to stress, however, that the city is a vibrant and exciting place to visit, although the fact that it covers just

0.00003% of the earth's surface means that statistically it is highly unlikely to be chosen as a landing spot even if alien intelligence is sufficiently advanced to allow an attempt to drop in actually to be made.

THE DEADLY GULF OF CORRYVRECKAN

In Gaelic the name of the narrow strait between the Hebridean islands of Jura and Scarba – *Coire Bhreacain* – describes a 'cauldron of the speckled seas'. It's an apt name for what is officially the world's third largest natural whirlpool, with waves of up to thirty feet high. As such it is subject to numerous Admiralty warnings. According to the *Scotsman* newspaper the Royal Navy considers it to be unnavigable by vessels, but no mention is made of one-legged swimmers, which perhaps explains why Bill Dunn, a local farmer and George Orwell's disabled brother-in-law, once dived in to become the first person ever to swim across it.

Skye's McDino

While dinosaur bones and fossils are nowhere exactly common, people have been unearthing them for centuries, but never, it seems, in Scotland. Not until 1982, anyway, when a footprint from an ornithopod was found on the Isle of Skye, and then again in 1994 when a possible cetiosaurus (or whale-lizard) femur was found on the same island. At this rate, according to Dr Neil Clark, a palaeontologist at the Hunterian Museum in Glasgow, it will take Scotland's fossil hunters 'over 200 years to collect a complete dinosaur'.

For anyone interested Skye is definitely the place to look, however. The island's famous Kilt rocks are middle-Jurassic or approximately 165 million years old, and already lucky amateurs have found bones from a ceratosaur, a bird-like carnivore, and a creature similar to a stegosaurus, and several more footprints. Unfortunately the richest seams are buried beneath a hard volcanic layer, 100 feet thick in places, meaning that even now, millions of years after the creatures died out, the only practical way to find a fossil is to sit tight and wait for the rock to wear away so that it falls out.

LOCH NESS MONSTER: FACT OR FICTION?

A unique survivor of a species of long-lived plesiosaur, Britain's own bigfoot or just a harmful mix of hoax and wishful thinking? In truth neither the locals nor Scotland's tourist chiefs know any more about Nessie than the rest of us, and they probably prefer not to pry too deeply anyway for fear of killing the monster that lays the golden eggs.

If the beast does exist, it's certainly chosen the right place to hide. Loch Morar might be a bit deeper at its deepest point, Loch Lomond has a greater surface area and Loch Awe is indeed slightly longer. But Loch Ness has the greatest average depth and that means by far the greatest volume of water in which to hide. In fact, it is the largest loch by such a margin that at approximately ten *trillion* gallons (or nearly one and three-quarter cubic miles) it holds almost twice as much water as every lake in England and Wales put together.

The first supposed sighting of the not-so-wee beastie might have been as early as the 6th century; the first snap was taken in 1933; and in 1975 the naturalist Sir Peter Scott claimed to have found something huge in the deep waters. Unfortunately the name he gave it, *Nessiteras rhombopteryx*, was quickly outed as an anagram of 'Monster hoax by Sir Peter S', since which time the absence of any physical remains – and the fact that sonar has mapped every inch of the loch bottom and found nothing – has led the scientific community to dismiss the existence of a creature, let alone a whole colony.

Needless to say, this has had no impact whatsoever on the Nessie legend, nor prevented several rival lochs from coming up with cryptids of their own. At the last count nearly a dozen of them – Arkaig, Awe, Linnhe, Lochy, Lomond, Maree, Morar, Oich, Quoich, Shiel and Suainaval – were being promoted as the watery homes of unlikely beasts. The best bet is that most of these are giant eels, or entirely made up.

Nature's Larder

In January 2013 seagulls wheeling over St Cyrus in Aberdeenshire were reportedly thrilled when four massive barrel-shaped pieces of lard drifted onto the beach at the local nature reserve. Incredibly, the lard was around seventy years old, the cargo of a merchantman sunk off the east coast by enemy action during the Second World War. Over the years the barrels have rotted away, and every few years the occasional big storm washes the brilliant white lard onto the coast. In the 1940s and 1950s the locals would collect it and boil it up to get the sand out, and apparently it still smells fresh beneath the barnacles. But these days no one seems prepared to risk eating any, except the gulls and the odd dog out walking with its owner.

Scotland's Biggest Natural-born Killer

The smallest wee beasties are frequently the deadliest, which is why according to some estimates half of all the people who have ever lived died of one mosquito-borne ailment or another. Close behind this comes the flea, in particular the Oriental rat variety *Xenopsylla cheopis*, which is credited with wreaking havoc across Europe in the mid-1300s.

At initial reports of what came to be known as the Black Death the Scots were delighted to hear about the carnage down south – 'the foule deth that Ynglessh men dyene upon' – and, smugly assuming it was a heavenly judgment on their enemies, decided to take advantage.

As they began planning an invasion from the forests of Selkirk, however, it rapidly became apparent that this creature was to be no respecter of boundaries. By 1350 the flea and the related pestilence were well established north of the border as well as south of it, one chronicler describing 'a strange and unwonted kind of death, in so much as the flesh of the sick was somehow puffed out and swollen, and they dragged out their earthly life for barely two days'. Precisely how many Scots it killed is unclear, but it was probably around 200,000 out of a population of one million. Possibly thanks to the cold weather this was only about half the likely mortality rate experienced in England over the same period, but it was still a devastating blow, and sufficient to make it the worst calamity ever to strike the Scottish people. So much for that tiny little flea . . .

THE REAL TOP TEN PEAKS

Much is made of Ben Nevis, and with good reason, but Scotland boasts not just the tallest peak in Britain but more than fifty of the tallest. As the following list shows, Snowdon falls well short of Scotland's top ten, at just over 3,500 feet, and England's Scafell Pike is hardly worth a mention at 3,209 feet.

Ben Nevis	(4,409 feet)
Ben Macdui	(4,295 feet)
Braeriach	(4,252 feet)
Cairn Toul	(4,236 feet)
Sgòr an Lochain Uaine	(4,127 feet)
Cairn Gorm	(4,081 feet)
Aonach Beag	(4,049 feet)
Aonach Mòr	(4,006 feet)
Càrn Mòr Dearg	(4,003 feet)
Ben Lawers	(3,983 feet)

Britain's highest mountains, those over 3,000 feet, are classified as Munros after a list compiled in 1891 by the peak-bagging baronet Sir Hugh Munro (1856–1919) for the *Scottish Mountaineering Club Journal*.

Subject to change from time to time as surveying techniques improve (for a long while it was thought that Ben Macdui was higher than Ben Nevis), the list currently comprises 283 peaks and to date some 4,000 mountaineers have bagged the lot. Sadly this is something Sir Hugh failed to do, as he fell victim to the devastating Spanish flu pandemic. This killed around fifty million worldwide and bagged Sir Hugh before he had climbed to the 3,091-feet summit of Carn Cloich-Mhuillin in the Cairngorms.

The Munros' little brothers are called Corbetts, Scottish hills of between 2,500 feet and 3,000 feet, of which at the time of writing there are 221, and then come the 224 Grahams at between 2,000 feet and 2,500 feet. Donalds are 2,000 feet and over, and the smallest – and therefore the largest category of all – are the Marilyns, a group of peaks of 500 feet. There are more than 2,000 in the whole of the British Isles, of which just over 1,200 are in Scotland.

3

Tourist Scotland

'Many of them were Scotchmen in their plaids and their music was delightful. Even the bagpipe was not disagreeable.'

John Adams (1735–1826),
2nd President of the United States of America

South-west Scotland

Most know Llanfairpwllgwyngyllgogerychwyrndrobwyll-llantysiliogogogoch as the longest, but few can name **the shortest place name in Britain**. In fact it is Ae, a small village that lies near the Water of Ae, a tributary of the River Annan. Scotland also has places called Dallas, California, Houston, Lamancha, Patna, Moscow, Bolton, Towie and even Lost (which is in Aberdeenshire). The one with the most unpronounceable name is probably the tiny village of Achluachrach near Invergarry, and in 2012 to the great delight of headline writers it was announced that Dull (in Perthshire) was twinning with Boring, which is in Oregon.

A **surprising subtropical enclave,** Logan Botanical Garden near Drummore was established in the 19th century and is now an offshoot of the Royal Botanic Garden of Edinburgh. On a peninsula jutting out into the Irish Sea, the warming effect of the Gulf Stream has enabled a variety of exotic species to thrive including gunnera from Brazil, colourful rhododendrons – of which the RBG has the world's largest collection – and Kiwi cabbage palms.

Situated about ten miles from Wigtown, the ruins at Whithorn – from 'white house' – are the last surviving remnants of **Scotland's earliest recorded Christian settlement.** Born locally, St Ninian travelled to Rome and after being made a bishop was sent back in AD 397 to convert his people.

Famously the only place in Britain where **motorists can roll uphill,** the logic-defying stretch of the A719 north of Govan is sadly only an optical illusion – something to do with the configuration of the surrounding landscape. For a long time the cause was assumed to be something mysterious and magnetic, hence its local nickname of 'Electric Brae', from the Scottish for hill.

You'd think **Scotland's highest village** would be in the Highlands, but in fact, at 1,380 feet, the settlement of Wanlockhead is to be found in the Lowther Hills in Dumfries and Galloway.

Having recently celebrated its 300th birthday, Sanquhar in Dumfriesshire boasts the **world's oldest post office.** Predating rivals in Chile and Sweden by decades, it also beat the beginnings of a uniform penny post service by well over a century.

Actually a **gigantic glacial feature from the Ice Age,** the wonderfully named Whangie – a 300-foot-long gash in a hillside at Carbeth north of Glasgow – is sometimes attributed to the devil, who left a visible scar when he whipped his tail across the hillside. Around fifty feet deep, it provides a popular challenge for local climbers.

South-east Scotland

Decommissioned shortly after the Berlin Wall came down, **Scotland's largest nuclear bunker** – or at least the largest one the authorities are owning up to – lies approximately 100 feet under a field outside Troywood near St Andrews. Extending over more than 24,000 square feet, and reached through a tunnel more than 400 feet long, it is protected by ten feet of concrete, blastproof doors and many hundreds of tons of shock-absorbing gravel. In 2004 one Ronald McDonald attempted to break in, being of no fixed abode and armed with a JCB digger, but these days visitors are welcome on payment of just £6.95 or £3.95 for children. (For more on this kind of thing, see the Secret Scotland chapter.)

The **world's first rotating boat lift,** the ingenious Falkirk Wheel is an elegantly engineered solution to the problem of transferring boats to a modern aqueduct from a 200-year-old canal situated more than 100 feet below. Able to lift eight vessels at a time – and replacing a time-consuming flight of eleven locks – it is so beautifully balanced that a half-turn uses no more power than eight domestic kettles. That said, its official opening in 2002 was sadly delayed by a month when vandals inflicted more than £350,000 of damage on the machinery used to operate it. It has since appeared on the reverse of the Scottish £50 note.

An early example of *nouveau riche* bling, James Miller was the son of a Victorian herring merchant who married the sister of the Indian Viceroy. To impress his new in-laws, in 1893 he decided to update his house, telling the architect to spend whatever he wished. The result was Scotland's **only silver staircase,** together with columns of the rarest, most expensive marble, an embarrassment of gold leaf and walls hung with silk. Fantastically vulgar – in the stables the name of each horse (all beginning with M) was engraved on a marble plaque – but age has fortunately mellowed Manderston House near Duns, which these days is open to the public and home to **the world's largest private collection of Huntley and Palmer biscuit tins**.

Thought to be the **world's oldest national frontier,** Carter Bar on the A68 has marked the boundary between two kingdoms since AD 1018. Sandwiched as it is between rugged moorland to the south and the gentle landscape of the borders, it is by far the most beautiful place to cross from Scotland into England, and close to the site of the Redeswire Raid of 1575, **the last major battle between the two nations**.

A strange museum stowaway came to light in 1994 when a builder engaged to knock down a wall at Edinburgh's Royal Museum of Scotland spotted something in the stonework. Closer examination revealed the fossilised remains of a 336-million-year-old swamp tree in the sandstone, a lycopsid or scale tree that was traced to Hermand Quarry in West Lothian, where it would have flourished during the Carboniferous era. At this time Scotland was situated close to the equator and such trees grew to more than 110 feet in height.

Edinburgh's former Craiglockhart military hospital, the celebrated meeting place of Great War poets Wilfred Owen and Siegfried Sassoon, is home to **Scotland's rarest fungus**. Scientists believe that *Clavulinopsis cinereoides*, which is found nowhere else in the United Kingdom, travelled here from the trenches on the boots of soldiers brought for treatment.

The **National Monument of Scotland**, on Edinburgh's Calton Hill, was intended as 'A Memorial of the Past and Incentive to the Future Heroism of the Men of Scotland' and designed to echo the Parthenon in Athens. Work began in 1826 but then stopped again three years later when the money ran out. Just twelve columns had been completed, the city having raised just £16,000 when £42,000 was required, and work was never resumed.

The 450-year-old Fernie Castle Hotel in Fife has a **unique guest suite housed in a treehouse** located high up in between six lofty sycamore trees.

In Dunfermline's Moodie Street the **birthplace of Andrew Carnegie** provides chapter one of an astonishing autobiography in architecture. Compare this rough stone cottage with the grandeur of Skibo Castle, which the great philanthropist built for himself in Sutherland sixty-odd years later, and it paints an extraordinary picture of one man's journey from poverty to becoming conceivably the world's richest man. Believing that 'the man who dies thus rich dies disgraced', he gave away nine-tenths of his fortune before his death in 1919, the remaining 10% being distributed to charitable foundations and pensioners shortly afterwards.

At Galashiels in the Borders a new sculpture has been erected to honour **the ugliest woman in Scotland**. Muckle Mou'd Meg was the daughter of 17th-century nobleman Sir Gideon Murray, the king's treasurer. Unable to marry her off, he offered her to a convicted cattle rustler who said she was so ugly he'd rather hang for his crimes. He nearly did but changed his mind on seeing the gallows and despite her hideous countenance the two are said to have enjoyed a long and happy marriage.

Central Scotland

Half a dozen miles east of Inverness, cold, bleak Culloden Moor marks the site of an **infamous massacre** where 5,500 troops under Bonnie Prince Charlie met as many as 9,000 troops commanded by the Duke of Cumberland, George I's younger son. Known as 'Sweet William' or 'the Butcher' depending on your sympathies, in 1746 the duke oversaw the killing of many hundreds of Scots troops, the execution for treason of some clan chiefs, and the suppression of many aspects of traditional Highland life.

In Inverness itself the local maritime museum includes the **world's largest model of the *Titanic*.** The town has no formal connection with the famous vessel, except that a local unemployed man spent more than a decade building the 100-foot replica before putting it on display in time for the centenary commemoration of the ill-fated liner.

Besides Britain's highest peak in Ben Nevis (at 4,406 feet) – first scaled by car when an Edinburgh dealer made the trek in his Model T Ford in 1911 – this region is also home to **the deepest lake in the British Isles**. Loch Morar, whose depths plunge to 1,107 feet, is easily deep enough to sink Europe's tallest building, and has its own Nessie-type monster. Known as Morag, she 'appears in a black heap or ball slowing and deliberately rising in the water and moving along like a boat water-logged'. Though often described as looking almost selkie- or mermaid-like, with flowing white hair and prominent breasts, the creature is considered in much the same way as the grim reaper, with every sighting heralding a death in the area.

Opposite Elgin Cathedral, **Britain's only biblical garden** contains examples of every plant species mentioned by name in the Bible, a total of 110, together with sculptures depicting various stories from the Testaments, Old and New, including the Good Shepherd, the Prodigal Son and Moses and the Ten Commandments.

The Findhorn Foundation near Kinloss, Britain's **oldest New Age community**, continues to thrive after more than fifty years. In a combination of caravans and more sophisticated eco-homes, some eighty or so residents live sustainably while promoting various alternative lifestyles through education and example as well as by hosting cultural events.

Located to the west of Aberdeen and reckoned to be **the largest man-made hole in Europe**, Rubislaw Quarry opened in 1740 and was sold a few years later for just £13. The low price reflected the supposedly poor quality of the granite quarried there, stone that for more than 200 years has nevertheless provided outstanding building materials for much of Aberdeen as well as London's Waterloo Bridge, the terraces for the Houses of Parliament and the Forth Rail Bridge. Nearly 500 feet deep, and last quarried in 1971, it is now full of water.

Still in Aberdeen, the city's **Central Library, the church of St Mark and His Majesty's Theatre** all stand in a row when viewed from Union Terrace. Because of this the locals refer to the trio as 'Education, Salvation and Damnation'.

A **thousand-year-old monolith** now housed in a stylish, modern glass enclosure, Sueno's Stone near Forres dates from around AD 900. More than twenty feet high, the richly carved red sandstone is thought to depict a battle victory of Christian Scots over a heathen tribe of Picts. It shows cavalry charges as well as archers and grisly decapitations, and is also said to be where **Macbeth met the three witches**, although this seems less likely.

Scotland's smallest distillery, Edradour in Pitlochry, produces just 90,000 litres of malt whisky annually yet welcomes 100,000 visitors through the doors.

South of Aviemore, Rothiemurchas Forest is a unique and important natural survivor. It is **a remnant of the great Caledonian forest** that grew up after the last Ice Age, but which over the last 8,000 years has been gradually swept away by the need for grazing land, timber and fuel. Rocky outcrops and a rich undergrowth have made it one of the last refuges for wild cats and red squirrels.

A splendid example of **sea-carved rocks**, the deep red sandstone of Seaton Cliffs at Arbroath has been sculpted into wonderful organic forms by the force of nature. A walk of almost three miles takes in several spectacular features, including the Needle E'e – a hole in an otherwise solid rock wall – a storm-washed stack called De'il's Heid, and the natural arch known as the Dark Cave, as well as blowholes and smugglers' caverns.

The supposed **grave of Queen Guinevere** is located about five miles from Coupar in Angus. Her 9th-century monument is one of more than two dozen Pictish stones in the Meigle Carved Stone Museum and appears to show her being torn to pieces by animals on the orders of an envious and vengeful King Arthur.

Near Meikleour on the A93 Perth-Blairgowrie road, the **world's tallest hedge** dates back to 1745. Working on an estate owned by the Marquess of Lansdowne, Robert Murray-Nairne, one of the fallen of Culloden (see above), planted a hedge of beech saplings more than 1,700 feet in length. Since his death it has grown to a height of around 100 feet, and is also the longest hedge anywhere in Britain.

Scotland's only lake is the Lake of Menteith near Aberfoyle, or rather it would be were it not merely the result of a cartographer's mistake. The name actually comes from 'laich', meaning a low-lying area.

Britain's tallest tree, by the way, is at Dunkeld, a 212-foot-high Douglas fir, while **Europe's oldest tree** is thought to be a heavily twisted yew in Fortingall. It is believed to have stood here for 3,000 years, maybe as many as 5,000, and locals like to think that Pontius Pilate was born in its shade and played beneath it as a child.

Hidden deep inside Ben Cruachan near Dalmally, Scotland's **greenest power station** required the excavation of more than six million cubic feet of rock and mud from inside the mountain to create a man-made void the height of a seven- or eight-storey building with a floor area equal to a football pitch. The machinery itself produces forty-four million watts of electricity using gravity and water, and in times of low demand pumps everything backwards to replenish its high reservoir with water from Loch Awe. Nicknamed Hollow Mountain, the site was used as a location for the James Bond film *The World is not Enough*.

The North Highlands and Beyond

Continuously inhabited from 2500 BC until the 17th century, the settlement of Jarlshof in Shetland includes Bronze and Iron Age remains as well as Pictish art, Viking ruins and a fortified medieval stone farmhouse. Incredibly it is still not a World Heritage Site, perhaps because, as an American tourist is said once to have remarked, 'they built it too close to airport' (Lerwick's runway is next door).

The colourful and richly ornate interior of the Italian Chapel on Lamb Holm in the Orkneys looks like stone but is a fake constructed inside a pair of Army Nissen huts. It was built by **Italian prisoners of war** in the 1940s, a group of nearly 600 men brought to the island as a means of preventing their escape. In direct contravention of the Geneva Convention they were put to work on the Royal Navy's Churchill Barriers around Scapa Flow – crucial defences not actually completed until four days after the German surrender – and created the chapel in their spare time as a reminder of their homeland.

Everyone knows about John O'Groats, or thinks he does, but **the most northerly point** on the Scottish mainland is actually wild and windy Dunnet Head some twelve miles away.

With just under 800 islands, 130 of which are inhabited, Scotland also boasts the **world's shortest scheduled commercial airline route.** This is the one-and-a-half-miles-long flight from Westray to Papa Westray in the Orkneys, a journey that typically takes just one minute and fourteen seconds to complete.

Just as nuclear submarines shelter in fortified pens at Faslane, so Smoo Cave near Durness once provided another **secret underground bunker**, this time for Viking raiders to conceal their ships. A vast sea cave more than 100 feet deep, Smoo has been compared to a cathedral as well as to Jonah's whale. It reaches to a lake behind which is fed by a waterfall that thunders in from a sinkhole in the landscape up above.

Beauly railway station, the first stop on the line from Inverness heading north on the Kyle of Lochalsh line, has a platform that is only long enough for a single coach. This makes it **the smallest railway station in Britain**, although it still serves approximately 1,000 passengers a week.

The Highlands could soon have its own **Statue of Liberty** if the owner of the 65,000-acre Balnagowan estate near Kildary in Ross-shire gets his way. Convinced that Scots are all descended from a mysterious Egyptian princess, businessman Mohammed Fayed has offered to present his adopted country with a gigantic sculpture of Scota, daughter of Pharoah Chencres, if and when Scotland votes for independence.

A **vast cavern** more than 220 feet long, 40 feet wide and 60 feet high, Fingal's Cave on the island of Staffa is formed by hexagonal basalt columns similar to those that make up the Giant's Causeway in Northern Ireland. As well as inspiring the composer Felix Mendelssohn, who visited in 1829 – in Gaelic the name *An Uaimh Bhinn* means 'the melodious cave' – the area has an unexpected European connection as the Swiss town of Stäfa was named by a monk from nearby Iona.

Bealach na Bà is only **Britain's third highest road** but, rising to more than 2,000 feet above Loch Kishorn in Wester Ross, it is high enough to thrill and probably the most challenging. Gradients are as steep as 1:5, and motorists ignoring the warning signs at the foot have encountered blizzards in summer. At the same time its snaking hairpins make the drive infinitely more interesting than anything you'll find on the highest, the Cairnwell Pass on the main A93.

Neptune's Staircase near Fort William on the Caledonian Canal is **the longest stairlock system in the British Isles**. Devised by Thomas Telford (1757–1834), there are eight locks in all, each capable of taking an ocean-going vessel and closed by two pairs of gates weighing twenty-two tons apiece. When it was hand-powered, traversing all eight used to take half a day; today, with hydraulic power replacing human, it can be achieved in around 90 minutes.

By contrast the **shortest street in Britain** is Ebenezer Place in Wick, Caithness. At just six feet nine inches long and completed in 1887, it contains only one address, at No. 1, which is the door to a restaurant forming part of a hotel in an adjacent street.

It's possible to take a sleeper train as far as Inverness. Additionally visitors to Rogart in Sutherland can **sleep aboard a train** by booking accommodation in one of three old railway carriages and a bus that have been converted to provide beds for up to twenty-six guests.

Finally, if you fancy **a second Christmas lunch**, islanders on Foula still celebrate it according to the old Julian calendar, so that Christmas Day is 6 January and New Year's Eve 12 January.

4

Transport Scotland

'What was wrong with train toilet doors that just locked, instead of this multiple choice system? If anything goes wrong, you'll be sitting there while the whole toilet wall slowly slides away, unveiling you like a prize on a quiz show.'

Frankie Boyle, Glaswegian stand-up

Scotland's Greatest Cars

Back in 1914 there were at least 50 different car makers north of the border, and Edinburgh's Caledonian Hotel offered a special 'chauffeur's rate' of only 7/6d (37.5p) for bed, breakfast, lunch and dinner. Since then it's true to say Scotland has rarely troubled the global motor industry, although there have been a few interesting contributions over the years if anyone cares to recall them . . .

AC 3000ME

This short-lived V6-engined two-seater was produced in Hillingdon near Glasgow in the mid-1980s. There were plans to build around 400 a year of them using Alfa Romeo engines, but probably no more than thirty were completed before the money ran out. Production then moved back to England where, curiously, it was renamed the AC Ecosse.

Argyll 12.4

This was built at a factory at Bridgeton, Glasgow, until 1906 when the company moved to the huge new Alexandria Works in West Dunbartonshire. Too huge might be a better description, as the plant covered more than twelve acres and had a palatial 500-foot façade of sandstone, granite and Italian marble; also its own railway line, but hardly any customers. Within two years the boss was dead, the company nearly bankrupt, and the factory transferred to the Admiralty to build torpedoes. Today it's a shopping centre.

Argyll GT Turbo

No relation to the above, this mid-engined sports car was produced at Lochgilphead from the late 1970s. Though oddly proportioned (i.e. ugly) it handled well and was certainly fast. Unfortunately it reportedly cost more than a Porsche 911, despite being a bit of a mongrel with a choice of Saab or Renault engines, Triumph steering wheel and suspension, and other bits pinched from the Morris Marina.

Arrol-Johnston

Self-declared to be among 'the finest cars ever built in the world', the A-J was produced in Glasgow by George Johnston, the first Scottish motorist to be charged, prosecuted and fined after driving his car around St Enoch's Square in 1896. Completed in 1912, his new factory was the first in Britain to be built using reinforced concrete, but soon afterwards closed as the company failed to compete with the cheap mass-production techniques of William Morris down in Oxford.

Beardmore

Primarily a Clydeside shipbuilder, the company also built biplanes and railway locomotives before branching out into cars in 1917. With a plant at Anniesland and later Paisley, its most successful model was a taxi, prompting a move to Hendon in north London where production continued until 1966. The founder William Beardmore, later Lord Invernairn, gave his name to the mighty Beardmore Glacier in Antarctica and at one point employed more than 50,000 Scots making everything from airships to pre-fabricated houses.

Craigievar Express

More of a wagon than a motor car, among the prized exhibits at Aberdeen's Grampian Museum of Transport is a primitive steam-driven cart invented by the local postman to help him on his round.

Galloway

An offshoot of Arrol-Johnston, the Galloway hailed from Tongland near Kirkudbright, and if the advertising could be believed the cars were all built 'by ladies for ladies'. In 1921 the boss was a woman, and there were certainly more on the shop floor than at your average car plant. Unfortunately there was little appetite for what was essentially a smaller, cheaper A-J, and the factory closed for good after barely two years.

Hillman Imp

Codenamed 'Slug', this surprisingly advanced design – one of the development engineers later raced for Ferrari – had a lightweight aluminium engine and looked sharply contemporary. Its reliability was hugely suspect, however, and like so much else in the 1960s it was steamrollered by the all-conquering Mini.

Madelvic

Formed in Edinburgh in January 1898, Sir William Peck's Madelvic Carriage Company boasted that it was the first British car company to have a purpose-built factory but was also, alas, the first to go into liquidation.

Neale

In 1897, at a time when petrol was by no means the default choice for pioneering automobilists, the Edinburgh entrepreneur Douglas Neale chanced his arm with electric propulsion. A price of £150 was high for the time, however – houses could be bought for less – and it is doubtful that he built more than four cars in all.

Parabug

Hoping to cash in on the 1970s dune buggy craze, this angular-looking kit car was designed by a boatbuilder in Tullos, Aberdeen, using the engine and chassis from an old VW Beetle. The fold-flat windscreen was held in place by magnets, but the off-road performance failed to match its jeep-like appearance.

Scamp

Produced by Scottish Aviation at Prestwick Airport, this 1965 oddball was another one powered by batteries rather than petrol, but with a top speed of 35 mph and a range of only twenty miles it was an idea that never caught on. Fifty years later, it still hasn't.

Talbot Sunbeam

Built at Linwood's old Imp plant, this compact hatchback was an also-ran until factory staff built a hot version in their spare time. A star was born when one of them dropped a 230-horsepower Lotus engine into the engine bay, and in 1981 it became the first and so far only Scottish car to win the World Rally Manufacturers' Championship.

Mazda MX5

Not quite Scottish, but in 1996 when Edinburgh-born Henry Wallace took over the top job in Hiroshima it was the first time a major Japanese company was headed by a foreigner.

WHERE LEFT IS RIGHT

The subject of a Papal Edict from Pope Boniface VIII (1235–1303), it was Scotland not England that pioneered driving on the wrong side of the road. This became a legal requirement north of the border as long ago as 1772, but England and Wales followed suit only in 1835. Sadly, almost no one else bothered besides the colonies and dominions, although Japan is still the most notable exception. (Sweden was too for a while, but in 1967 driving was banned for one whole weekend and by Monday morning the entire country had switched to driving on the right.)

Driving Round in Circles

Undeniably impressive, Scotland's contribution to motorsport in all classes has seen a relatively small population punching well above its weight.

- A three-time winner of the Le Mans 24 Hour race, **Alan McNish** was born in Dumfries and now lives in Monaco, although he included a Queen of the South match as part of his stag weekend celebrations.

- Born in Paisley without a right hand (his mother had German measles while pregnant), **Archie Scott Brown** never grew taller than five foot, but was a ferocious and effective competitor in both sports cars and Formula 1. He died in 1958 after crashing at Spa-Francorchamps.

- Brought up in Twynholm in Kirkcudbrightshire, **David Coulthard** twice won the Monaco Grand Prix wearing a distinctive blue helmet with a white saltire on the top.

- Racing in Formula 1 between 1965 and 1973, **Jackie Stewart** won three World Drivers' Championships. As a teenager he also triumphed in the English, Scottish, Irish and Welsh clay pigeon shooting championships, but inexplicably failed to make the Olympic squad.

- From a famous rallying dynasty, in 1995 Lanark-born **Colin McRae** became the first Briton to win the World Rally Championship. A hugely popular figure, he died young when a helicopter he was piloting plummeted to the ground in 2007.

- A four-time Indycar Series championship winner (and cousin to Formula 1 driver Paul di Resta), **Dario Franchitti** married Hollywood star Ashley Judd at Andrew Carnegie's Skibo Castle near Dornoch, but later divorced.

- Winner of the 1963 and 1965 Formula 1 World Drivers' Championships, Fife-born **Jim Clark** was buried in the village of Chirnside in Berwickshire after dying behind the wheel of his Lotus.

- **John Bute**, aka Johnny Dumfries, or more correctly the 7th Marquess of Bute, had a disappointing career in F1 partnering Ayrton Senna, but scored a popular victory in the 1988 Le Mans race driving a Jaguar.

- From 1983–1997 the aviation entrepreneur from Edinburgh **Richard Noble** was the fastest man on earth, having hit an astounding 633.468 mph in his *Thrust2* jet-powered car.

THE WEIRDEST SHIPS BUILT ON CLYDESIDE

1880: The world's first and last plaice-shaped royal yacht, the *Livadia* was built for Alexander II to a design by Vice-Admiral Popoff, Tsarist Russia's top naval architect. Some 253 feet long and more than 150 feet wide, it was hoped that the unorthodox shape would prevent the ship rolling, as the Tsarina was a martyr to seasickness. Unfortunately the Tsar was assassinated before the *Livadia* could even be launched and, converted to a coal hulk, his new yacht was eventually scrapped in 1926.

1899: The SS *Chauncey Maples* was broken up as soon as she was completed, then packed into boxes and shipped off to East Africa. Carried overland to Lake Nyasa (now Lake Malawi) – hauling the 11-ton boiler more than 300 miles took 450 men – all 3,481 components were then reassembled and the vessel launched onto the lake in 1901. Remaining in service for more than a century, she is currently undergoing restoration.

1968: HMS *Otway*. Following her decommissioning this Oberon class Cold War-era submarine has gone on display at a public park in Holbrook, New South Wales – or rather the top half has. It's not clear whether or not the town authorities wanted the entire vessel, but with the lower half missing it looks for all the world as though the sub has somehow surfaced in the middle of the town.

Twelve Bits of Scottish Railway Trivia

Altnabreac on the Far North line is famously the only mainline station in the UK with no road access, but then Scotland abounds in such peculiarities:

1. The Forth Rail Bridge was the first ever to be made of steel, and on its completion in 1890 also the largest bridge in the world. It weighs 72,250 tons, but in heavy rain this can go up by more than a hundred tons.
2. Building it took eight years, cost ninety-eight lives, and consumed approximately 6.5 million rivets and about ten times as much metal as the structurally similar but largely iron Eiffel Tower (whose creator incidentally, Gustav Eiffel, was present at the opening ceremony).
3. Scotland's oldest railway viaduct is the Laigh Milton near Kilmarnock (1812) while its highest, at 169 feet, is the Ballochmyle on the River Ayr. On its completion in 1848 the latter boasted the world's widest masonry arch at 181 feet.
4. Intended to link Aberdeen and Inverness in the 1840s (which actually it never did), the Great North Scottish Railway was the first to have an electric telegraph along its entire length. Curiously there were no second class coaches.
5. The North British Railway, which ran trains from Edinburgh to Berwick-on-Tweed from 1846, had a tartan-liveried locomotive and two special 'prison coaches' to transport convicts to Peterhead gaol.
6. For many years the general public considered train travel too hazardous to undertake. The turning point came in 1848 when Queen Victoria made a 500-mile journey herself, travelling by rail down from her first ever holiday on Deeside and in the process persuading ordinary people that it was probably safe.
7. Increased confidence notwithstanding, the Tay Bridge Disaster

of December 1879 killed an estimated seventy-five passengers and crew on board the Wormit to Dundee service. There were no survivors and thirty bodies were never found.

8. Among those who escaped an almost certain death at Tay Bridge were Karl Marx and Friedrich Engels, both of whom were planning to join the train but at the very last minute decided to stay an extra night in Edinburgh.

9. Scotland's only underground network, the Glasgow Subway, is the world's oldest after the London 'Tube' and the Budapest Metro.

10. The Caledonian Sleeper from London to Fort William and Inverness (also known as the 'Deerstalker') is one of only two sleeper services to survive in Britain. The other is the Night Riviera from London to Penzance.

11. Authorised by the Duke of Sutherland's Railway Act of 1870, the Golspie to Helmsdale line is still in use today and was built largely by the aforenamed nobleman to link his ancestral seat with the rest of the network. Driving his own locomotive, the duke entertained Queen Victoria, Edward VII, George V, George VI, King Alfonso of Spain and Kaiser Wilhelm II, and until 1949 the family enjoyed the unusual privilege of being able to hook up their own private, green-liveried luxury coach to passing mainline trains.

12. In 1848 when the Polish composer Frédéric Chopin arrived in Edinburgh it was by train. His sponsor, piano maker Henry Broadwood, had thoughtfully booked two seats, one for the maestro and one for his legs. (More on Broadwood in 'Inventing Scotland'.)

THE REAL FLYING SCOTSMAN

In 1930 George Bennie's Airspeed Railway – also known as the Railplane – aimed to separate fast passenger traffic from slower freight trains by running the former on overhead monorails powered by large, nine-foot-diameter four-bladed propellers.

It sounded like something dreamed up by W. Heath Robinson, but to Bennie's credit he had soon managed to design, fund and build a working, full-size prototype. This ran for a quarter of a mile over the disused LNER sidings to the Burnbrae Dyeworks at Milngavie near Glasgow, its single carriage an elegant, streamlined cigar shape. This was luxuriously appointed with stained glass, deep carpets, individual table lamps and curtained windows.

On 8 July sundry reporters and VIPs were offered a test-run, one of Bennie's guinea pigs noting that with its 'perfect smoothness, passengers only knew the car was moving by gazing out of the window at the passing landscape. There was no bumping over rails, smoke or whistle shrieking . . . a sheer delight.'

Hailed as 'a triumph of Great British Brains', the prototype won a gold medal at the Industrial Exhibition in Edinburgh amidst talk of a new high-speed line being built to link London's Victoria Station with Croydon Aerodrome in the Surrey suburbs. Sadly, sufficient funds were not forthcoming and by 1936 Bennie had been ousted from his own company. Undaunted, he formed a new company, George Bennie Airspeed Railway (Iraq) Ltd, proposing to combine passenger-carrying and desert irrigation services between the River Nile and the Dead Sea, Baghdad and Damascus.

In Scotland, meanwhile, the test track was dismantled, and in 1941 it was melted down as part of the wartime drive for metal. The exotic coach lay on its side rotting in a field until the 1950s, but eventually it too was scrapped, by which time Bennie had switched tracks himself and was running a shop selling herbal remedies.

Twelve Snippets of Scottish Aviation Trivia

1. The son of a Forfarshire Presbyterian minister, *Encyclopaedia Britannica* editor James Tytler (1745–1804) was the first person in Britain to fly in a balloon. At his first attempt on 25 August 1784 he rose just a few feet above Edinburgh, but subsequent ascents proved costly and in less than a year he was broke.

2. RAF Leuchars on the east coast is the oldest military airfield in the United Kingdom. Actually a full decade older than the RAF, it can trace its origins to 1908 when a Royal Engineers balloon squadron was based here.

3. High School of Dundee alumnus Sir Robert Lang Lickley (1912–1998) designed the 1956 Fairy Delta 2, the first aircraft in the world to exceed 1,000 mph.

4. Born in Glasgow to American parents, in 1919 Lt Col. Sir Arthur Whitten Brown, together with Capt. John Alcock, became the first man ever to fly non-stop across the Atlantic.

5. In 1933 the future 14th Duke of Hamilton, flying a Westland PV-3 biplane, was the chief pilot for the first flight over the top of Mt Everest.

6. Eight years later, when Rudolf Hess flew his Messerschmitt Bf 110 to Britain, the renegade Nazi managed to evade the RAF before parachuting onto the duke's Dungeval House estate and asking for him by name. (On being told that Hitler's deputy was under arrest in Scotland Prime Minister Winston Churchill expressed surprise but made no plans to alter his plans for the evening, which included watching the latest Marx Brothers film.)

7. Edinburgh airport, with its distinctive egg timer-shaped control tower, was developed from the Turnhouse Aerodrome, Britain's most northerly defence air base in the First World War.

8. Originally equipped for only the smallest biplanes, it saw its first paved runway laid down for Supermarine Spitfires in the

1940s. This was then extended to 6,000 feet to accommodate the early jet-age De Havilland Vampire FB.5 fighter-bomber.

9. Ready for lift-off, Virgin Galactic's Chief Pilot David Mackay grew up in Helmsdale in the Highlands and studied aeronautical engineering at the University of Glasgow. (He was beaten to the edge of space by Aberdonian Brian Binnie, who took charge of *SpaceShipOne* in 2004 to become the 434th person to leave the Earth's atmosphere – just – but the first Scot and only the second civilian space pilot in history.)

10. Voted the world's top airport in 2011, Port-adhair Bharraigh – Barra International – is the only airport in the world where scheduled flights use the beach as a runway. Pilots can accordingly only land and take off at low tide, and cockle-pickers are warned to keep an eye out for approaching aircraft.

11. Except during the weekend of the British Formula 1 Grand Prix (when it is briefly displaced by Silverstone), the offshore oil industry ensures that Aberdeen Airport is the world's busiest heliport.

12. Glasgow-born Wing Commander Norman Macmillan was the first pilot to land at Heathrow. Unfortunately when he did this it was an emergency landing in a field in 1925, more than twenty years before the airport opened for business.

A SMALL GLEN FOR A MAN, A GIANT LEAP FOR MANKIND

In 2012, when a vehicle of an entirely different kind finally touched down on Mars, the village of Glenelg in the western Highlands announced its intention to twin with its Martian namesake more than thirty-five million miles away.

The village shares its name with an area on the red planet that was due to be visited by NASA's pioneering Curiosity rover. To celebrate the connection the village planned a traditional *ceilidh* gathering and a visit by retired Space Shuttle astronaut Bonnie Jeanne Dunbar, who unveiled a new road sign outside the village announcing that it is 'Twinned with Mars'.

Ms Dunbar has appropriately strong Scottish roots – her paternal grandfather Charles Dunbar was born in Dundee, and he married Mary, who was born close to Gardenstown near Banff – but she considers herself American. Because of this Scotland's most stellar achievement so far is perhaps managing to land a piece of tartan on the moon. Back in November 1969 a small piece of MacBean tartan was carried onto *Apollo 12* by astronaut Alan Bean before being transferred to the lunar module *Intrepid*. After touchdown on the moon's surface and then a safe return a precious fragment was entrusted to the care of the Scottish Tartans Authority in Crieff, Perthshire.

Haggis Helping Police with Their Inquiries

A couple of years ago police were called to a railway station in Inverness when passengers reported finding a four-foot-tall haggis in the baggage compartment of their train. With its pink kilt and an 'honest sonsie face', the haggis had travelled more than 100 miles from Kirkcaldy in Fife before being taken into custody, where it was found to be made of papier-mâché. The story, though bizarre, is far from unique. As this chapter was being written a former teacher from Melvaig in Wester Ross was detained at Birmingham Airport after a haggis he was carrying set off a security alarm. Worryingly, the same scanner failed to detect his *sgian-dubh*, the short-bladed but still deadly knife traditionally worn as part of Highland dress, and the traveller was permitted to continue his journey to Dublin.

Next Stop Nowhere: Britain's Loneliest Bus Stop

When the BBC launched a quest to find Britain's remotest bus stop, the winner was found in the middle of nowhere on a stretch of exceptionally bleak moorland near Cape Wrath. Intended for hikers making their way to a bothy at Kearvaig, and not even on a proper road, it is served by a minibus that shuttles back and forth along eleven miles of track. This links the cape and Durness passenger ferry and is used more by military vehicles than any other kind. Here on the most north-westerly point of the British mainland there is, needless to say, no timetable, and minibuses call by appointment only.

5

Sporting Scotland

'The secret of my success over the 400 metres is that I run the first 200 metres as hard as I can. Then, for the second 200 metres, with God's help, I run harder.'

Eric Liddell,
Scottish Olympian

Besides the obvious ones, such as tossing the caber or weight-for-height, a number of international sporting activities are uniquely Scottish, or can trace their roots straight back to Scotland.

Olympic events such as the **shot put** and **hammer** clearly derive from the traditional Highland Games, which in turn build on competitions known to have taken place as early as the 1st century AD. Shot put became an Olympic sport at the first modern Olympiad in 1896, although women had to wait for more than half a century before the authorities allowed them to have a go. Hammer throwing, meanwhile, may well have been devised as a way round a 14th-century decree of Edward I's prohibiting Scots from possessing conventional weapons.

Curling may be 'chess on ice' for those who follow it, but it remains something of a mystery to the casual spectator, for whom it looks more like winter bowls. Of the 1.2 million players these days Canada boasts the most, and it first became an international Olympic sport back in 1924, but wherever it is played the game is still coloured by more than a tint of Scottishness:

- In 1565 a painting by Pieter Bruegel (the Elder) depicted a game between Dutch peasants, but the first written reference to the game predates this by nearly twenty-five years and was found in the archives of Renfrew Abbey.
- The governing 'Rules in Curling' were drawn up by the Grand Caledonian Curling Club, which was established in Edinburgh in 1838, but the oldest extant curling stone dates back to 1511.
- The Caledonian was honoured with a royal prefix in 1842 after Queen Victoria was treated to a demonstration by Clackmannanshire's lord lieutenant, the 3rd Earl of Mansfield, on the polished floor of the ballroom at Scone Palace.
- In the 1960s the sport made fleeting appearances in two iconic movies, *On Her Majesty's Secret Service* and *Help!* But, perhaps because 007 declines to join in during his visit to Blofeld's Swiss mountain-top lair (and one of the Beatles' stones turns out to be a bomb), it has never quite managed to capture the public's imagination.
- Though curling is one of very few Winter Olympic sports to be played indoors, the year's big match in Scotland, the Grand Match, used to be held on Stirling's Lake of Menteith. Unfortunately since 1979

changing weather conditions have meant the ice there has not been thick enough for outdoor play.

- The all-important sweeping brushes traditionally comprised bundles of corn-stalks. More recently these have been replaced by horse hair and hogs' hair, but despite experiments with iron stones the best ones are still made by Kays of Scotland (established in 1851) using Blue Hone granite. This is carefully 'harvested' from Ailsa Craig as blasting is no longer permitted in the environmentally sensitive island environment.

Like the Dutch with curling, **Gaelic Handball** is most closely associated with the Irish, but the first recorded instance of the game was also in Scotland. In 1427 King James I, an enthusiastic player, ordered a low window to be bricked up to enable a courtyard in his palace to be used for the game.

One of the precursors to international **ice hockey**, shinty or *camanachd* has been played in the Highlands and islands for so long that some authorities claim it has a longer history than Scotland itself. In the early days a lack of trees in the Western Isles necessitated the use of seaweed stalks instead of wooden hooks, and the game is thought to have travelled to Nova Scotia with emigrants from around 1800 onward.

Rugby is clearly an English game, but **rugby sevens** was devised in 1883 by a pair of Melrose butchers. Ned Haig and David Sanderson staged tournaments to raise money for their local rugby football club. These were highly popular but it took more than forty years for the game to spread south into England, where in 1926 a sevens tournament raised more than £1,600 for the King Edward VII Hospital for Officers. (Our own queen was born the same year, and it's still the hospital of choice for Her Majesty.)

European soccer's first **dug-out**, or the 'technical area' as one is these days supposed to call it, was installed at Aberdeen FC's Pittodrie stadium around 1931. Coach Donald Colman wanted somewhere to shelter while observing the game and taking notes on the players' performance. Prior to this coaches and managers had to sit in the grandstand with the fans.

When it comes to **long-distance walking** few could equal the commitment of Robert Barclay Allardice (1779–1854), who won 1,000 guineas in 1809 by walking one mile an hour for a thousand hours.

For all this, the pre-eminent Scottish sport – and sporting export – is of course **golf**. The Romans had something called *paganica*, the English their *pell-mell* – London's principal playing ground has since given its name to Pall Mall – the Dutch *het kolven*, and it is known that Ming Dynasty Chinese were also swinging angled sticks at small balls in an attempt to propel them into tiny holes. But the modern game almost certainly originated in Scotland, although it was banned by James II, whose 1457 edict demanded that 'golfe be utterly cried down and not to be used' in an attempt to get the male population concentrating on its archery. A quick reverse provided the impetus for its growing popularity, however, and with a founding date no later than 1574 the Old Course at St Andrews is today regarded around the world as the 'home of golf'.

SCOTLAND'S GREATEST-EVER
SPORTING HEADLINE – I

In 2000, when Inverness Caledonian Thistle stage-managed one of those occasional giant-killing upsets by beating Celtic in the Scottish Cup, subs down in London on the *Sun* newspaper pulled out all the stops to come up with the truly eye-Poppins headline: SUPER CALEY GO BALLISTIC, CELTIC ARE ATROCIOUS.

Twelve Bits of Scottish Golfing Trivia

- Mary, Queen of Scots, is the first woman known to have played golf, and in 1567 she was censured for playing a round too soon after the murder of her husband Lord Darnley.

- An obelisk above the Old Course at St Andrews commemorates a number of Catholic martyrs who were burned on the site in the mid-1500s.

- The Royal and Ancient Club was established in 1754 by twenty-two gentlemen players who in those days wore a kind of semi-military uniform while playing. This was ten years after Muirfield's rival Honourable Company of Edinburgh Golfers, but in 1834 St Andrews edged ahead in terms of prestige after receiving its royal prefix as a gift from William IV. Until 1913 anyone could play here free of charge, and locals still could until 1946. (Today they enjoy the privilege of a reduced fee.)

- In the 1840s, with bankruptcy hanging over St Andrews, the land was used commercially to raise rabbits for the table.

- For many years, to the very great irritation of players, the town's residents used to lay their linen out on the greens in order to bleach it.

- The course originally had just eleven holes, which were played out and back again. This was cut to nine holes in 1764 – meaning a round comprised eighteen in total – and it was not until 1832 that the course finally gained eighteen separate holes.

- Clubs around the world eventually made the same change because the Royal and Ancient codified the game, and thus established all the rules.

- The green for the eighteenth hole lies over an old graveyard.

- The first Open at St Andrews was in 1873, the same year that the traditional claret jug trophy was introduced.

- Even now, no game is allowed to be played on the Old Course on Sundays.

- Golf's first prodigy, 'Old' Tom Morris, won the British Open four times in the 1860s. Unfortunately one Sunday in 1908, after enjoying a couple of pints of beer, he made his way towards the gents' but fell into the club's coal cellar and died shortly afterwards.

- Despite green fees of more than £150, guests today account for approximately 40% of Old Course players.

SCOTLAND'S GREATEST-EVER SPORTING
HEADLINE – II

In late April 1964, following an unusually high-scoring afternoon in the Scottish Second Division, some poor unfortunate sports announcer was left to deal with the tongue-twisting final result, FORFAR: 5, EAST FIFE: 4. The match had been played at Forfar Athletic's ground, Station Park, which despite the name enjoys the distinction of being further from a railway station than any other league ground in in Scotland with the exception of Peterhead's Balmoor stadium.

Twelve Bits of Scottish Soccer Trivia

- The first Scottish national side was composed entirely of players from Queen's Park FC, Scotland's oldest team. Now the only amateur side in the Scottish Professional Football League, Queen's Park is also the only Scottish team to have played in the FA Cup Final, a feat it achieved twice in the 1880s.

- Scotland has played in only eight World Cups despite qualifying nine times. In 1950 the decision was taken not to send a team to Brazil as Scotland were not the British champions.

- In 1937 for a Scotland v England match an incredible 149,415 spectators packed into Hampden Park. This was a European record, and still stands.
- Slightly more recently, in 1972, Scotland played in front of 130,000 fans at Rio's Maracana stadium. They lost 1–0 to Brazil following an 80th-minute goal by the legendary Jairzinho (aka Jair Ventura Filho).
- The team's most resounding victory was an 11–0 scoreline when playing against the Republic of Ireland in 1901 . . .
- . . . and its biggest defeat was going down 7–0 to Uruguay, the defending champions in the 1954 World Cup.
- Between 1881 and 1951 Scotland occasionally played in primrose and pink instead of dark blue. These were the racing colours of Archibald Philip Primrose, the 5th Earl of Rosebery, who was a former Liberal prime minister and honorary president of the Scottish Football Association.
- With 102 in his cupboard Kenny Dalglish is the only player of the men's game to exceed 100 caps for Scotland. He was in the team from 1971–1986, but his record is comfortably exceeded by Celtic's Gemma Fay, who at the time of writing had amassed a total of 162.
- Together with the exceptionally long-serving striker Denis Law (playing 1958–1974), Dalglish is also the country's top scorer in international games with thirty goals to his credit. Even he can't match Steve Archibald, however, who once appeared twice on *Top of the Pops* in a single night (with Tottenham Hotspur FC and the Scotland World Cup squad).
- Old-timer Hugh Kilpatrick 'Hughie' Gallacher (a team member from 1924–35) had a far better match average than any of these chaps, however, or indeed Miss Fay. Scoring 23 goals in just 20 games, he also holds the record for the most goals scored by a single player in a single match, since contributing five to a 7–3 victory over Northern Ireland in 1929.
- Between 1872 and 1929 Scotland played no truly international

fixtures, and against the home nations of England, Wales and Ireland she lost just two of the forty-two matches played.

- The first Scotsman to score a goal in an international match was Henry Renny-Tailyour in 1873. Still the only Scot to represent his country at both soccer and rugby, he also played first-class cricket for Kent.

CITIUS, FORTIUS, ALTIUS . . . SCOTIUS?

According to a recent survey 78% of Scots would like to see an independent Scottish Olympic team. Unfortunately the terms of the Olympic Charter expressly forbid the recognition of any team except from a sovereign nation, but this has not prevented a campaign being mounted to reverse the terms of the charter – nor done anything to dent Scotland's impressive performance over more than 100 years.

The **first Scottish Olympic medallist** was Launceston Elliot (1874–1930), who also became Britain's first Olympic champion after taking gold in the one-handed weightlifting at the Athens games in 1896. He tied first in the two-handed challenge as well, but was awarded silver, apparently only because King George of Greece thought the performance of his Danish rival was more stylish.

By far the **most successful Scottish Olympian** is cyclist Sir Chris Hoy. World champion eleven times, and Olympic champion six times, with a total of seven medals he is also is the most successful Olympic cyclist of all time.

Scotland's first female medallist was swimmer Isabella Moore (1894–1975) from Govan. At the 1912 Games in Stockholm she and three team mates from England and Wales took gold in the freestyle relay.

With their help the 1912 Games were **Scotland's most successful** so far, with a total of nine medals, including six

---

golds for running, rowing, shooting, water polo and swimming, and three silvers. This impressive tally remained unbeaten for 100 years, but in London in 2012 Scots won an astounding seven gold medals, four silver and three bronze.

Golf was included in the IInd Olympiad at Paris in 1900, but despite Scotland's long history with the game only two players were placed. Silver went to Walter Rutherford and David Robertson took the bronze.

The first Scottish runner to win an Olympic medal was Wyndham Halswelle of the Highland Light Infantry in 1904. Unfortunately his win in the 400 metres event at the London games four years later was so controversial that he quit soon afterwards. What became the **first ever Olympic walkover** occurred when Halswelle's American rival was disqualified by a British judge under circumstances so contentious that the rest of the field refused to run. Because of this Halswelle could literally have walked the course and still taken the gold.

The same year Halswelle set one of the **longest-standing Scottish records**. His time over 300 yards remained unbeaten until 1961 when it was overhauled by the future Olympian, British 100-metre record holder and sometime leader of the Liberal Democrats, Menzies Campbell.

The **first Scottish organisation** to win an Olympic medal was the Royal Northern and Clyde Yacht Club, which took Gold in the 12-metre class at the London Games in 1908. Now based in Rhu, the club dates back to 1824 and is thought to have been the first sailing club to gain a royal prefix.

George Thomson Cornet (1877–1952) was **the first Scot to win gold in two successive Games.** As a member of the Great Britain and Ireland water polo team he was victorious in London in 1908, and then again in Stockholm four years later.

The **first Scottish policeman to win an Olympic medal** was John Sewell from Half Moon in Dumfriesshire. This is worth mentioning only because in his chosen event – tug of war, in Stockholm in 1912 – the team members on both sides in the final were all rozzers.

Immortalised in the 1981 film *Chariots of Fire*, although not without some ruthless fact-bending, the religiously devout sprinter **Eric Liddell** is seen running on the beach a few miles north of St Andrews. In real life he won gold and bronze at the 1924 Paris Games before returning as a missionary to his birthplace in China. Imprisoned by the Japanese in 1943, he died five months before the internment camp was liberated. Because of this he is sometimes described as the first Chinese Olympian – if only by the Chinese – as he was born and died in that country.

When the **British hockey** team took silver at the 1948 Games in London five of the eleven players were Scots. They included the Scottish brothers Robin and William Lindsay and lost to India, a team that quite remarkably remained unbeaten from 1928 right through to 1960.

A commander of the Royal Scots Greys during the Second World War, Douglas Norman Stewart, DSO MC and Bar, was the **first Scottish equestrian medallist**. At Helsinki in 1952 he won Britain's only gold of the entire games.

Scotland's greatest swimmer, David Wilkie, won Gold in the 200 metres breaststroke at the Montreal Olympics in 1976. Significantly, his world-record time prevented what would otherwise have been an American clean sweep of all the men's swimming events.

In Moscow in 1980 Edinburgh-born sprinter Allan Wells became **the last white male athlete** to win the

Olympic 100 metres title. Multi-talented, he was also **Scottish long jump champion**, and in retirement coached the British bobsleigh team.

Quadruple silver medallist Ian Stark from Galashiels in the Borders won medals in the equestrian events in 1984, 1988 (team and individual) and 2000.

The first Scottish woman to win gold in two successive Olympic Games, Dundee-born Shirley Ann Robertson, sailed to victory in Sydney in 2000 and then again in Athens four years later. Also the first British woman to achieve the double in this way, she was subsequently voted **Female World Sailor of the Year.**

Scotland's first triple silver medallist is Edinburgh rower Katherine Grainger. Six-time World Champion, she won gold at the London Games in 2012 to become **Britain's most decorated female Olympian**, a title she shares with swimmer Rebecca Adlington.

Ahead of his historic, headline-grabbing victory at Wimbledon in 2013, Glasgow-born Andy Murray also became the **first Scottish Olympic tennis champion** having won both gold (singles) and silver (mixed doubles) at the 2012 Games. Wonder if he ever got to play at Falkland Palace, which has the **world's oldest real tennis court**, dating back to 1539? (Hampton Court had one first, admittedly, but its court was extensively refitted in the 1660s.)

When it comes to the **Winter Olympics**, it has to be said that Britain is generally pretty rubbish. In 1924, however, the Royal Caledonian Curling Club took gold at Chamonix, and twelve years later at Garmisch-Partenkirchen the Scottish-Canadian James Foster helped Britain win its first and only ice hockey gold.

Scots also made up the whole of the **winning ladies' curling team** at Salt Lake City in 2002, and at Sochi in

2014 it was Lockerbie that had the most to crow about. With three curling medallists among its residents, David Murdoch took silver after the men's team reached the final, while Anna Sloan and Claire Hamilton picked up bronzes.

More Sedentary than Sporting

The Scots didn't invent chess, but the Scottish Championship is the longest continual national event in the board game-playing world and was established in 1884. The country can also claim the world's oldest chess set, or rather it could were not nearly all of the seventy-eight pop-eyed pieces found in 1831 on the Isle of Lewis owned by the British Museum in London. Mostly of walrus ivory (a few are made from whale teeth), these were carved in Norway in the 12th century before somehow winding up buried in a sand bank at the head of Camas Uig on the island's west coast.

SCOTLAND'S GREATEST-EVER ALL-ROUNDER

Who now remembers Leslie Melville Balfour-Melville (1854–1937), who played rugby for Scotland in 1871, captained Scotland when they beat Australia at cricket in 1882, and was British Amateur Golf Champion for 1895? He was also Scottish billiards champion, won the Scottish Lawn Tennis Championship in 1879, and was pretty handy with a pair of ice-skates. Such is fame . . .

6

Secret Scotland

'The bunker – as an ex-Cold War facility – lends itself very well to being the council's emergency centre in the 21st Century.'

Highland Council spokesman, speaking in 2012

Behind Closed Doors:
Scotland's Top Secret Locations

- **11 Newbattle Terrace, Edinburgh.** In recent years it has been revealed that this is the secret location to which the Scottish arm of the BBC would have relocated had Britain had been invaded by Germany in 1940. From this otherwise anonymous address a skeleton staff operating from two small 'crisis' studios would have broadcast messages of defiance to organised resistance groups across the country. The work would have formed part of a nationwide secret radio network run from a bunker buried hundreds of miles away deep beneath the Essex countryside.

- **12 Drumsheugh Gardens, Edinburgh.** A private boarding house in 1914, this was where Carl Lody (posing as American tourist Charles A. Inglis) stayed while travelling by bicycle to observe shipping in the Firth of Forth. Arrested when his movements aroused suspicion, he was found in possession of incriminating notes and German gold. After a court martial in London he was shot at dawn, the first execution at the Tower of London since the Jacobite rebel Lord Lovat's beheading in 1747. In all, eleven spies were despatched in this way, meaning there were more executions at the Tower during the Great War than during the whole of the Tudor period.

- For more than sixty years **MoD Inchterf** near Kirkintilloch in East Dunbartonshire was a secretive proving range for testing guns and propellant charges at a rate of up to 45,000 bangs per annum. Established in the 1930s by William Beardmore of taxi fame (see Transport chapter), the facility could test weapons of up to twelve-inch calibre, but with firing controlled from a long blast-proof building anything larger risked damaging civilian property in Milton of Campsie. Ordnance and supplies arrived via a private railway line, but this no longer exists and the site is now being redeveloped as a light industrial estate.

- The village of **Arrochar** in Argyll and Bute was home to a classified Royal Navy torpedo testing range from 1912 until the late 1980s, with many thousands of weapons being fired the length of nearby Loch Long. In 1915 a Uruguayan with German family connections was arrested within hours of arriving in the area and found to be in possession of a map, a revolver, ammunition and some invisible ink. Identified as Augusto Alfredo Roggen, he too was promptly removed to the Tower of London where he was executed by a firing squad made up of men of the 3rd Battalion, The Scots Guards.

- **Greenock Cemetery** in the town's South Street was selected in February 1940 as the burial place for the bodies of twenty-five

German crewmen killed when their U-boat sank in the Firth of Clyde. Besides the loss of life the incident is significant because it led to the successful capture of three wheels from submarine *U-33*'s Enigma machine. Dramatically hastening the work of the Bletchley Park cryptographers, who had so far failed to crack the German naval codes, this was the first British breakthrough in the vitally important work needed to read German naval signals. The achievement is credited to an exceptionally sharp-eyed rating who spotted the sub's periscope from the deck of HMS *Gleaner*, a converted survey ship that was patrolling in the area.

- **Achnacarry House** in the Highlands was the historic seat of Clan Cameron. This 19th-century country house on the isthmus between lochs Lochy and Arkaig was requisitioned by the military authorities early on in the Second World War and re-cast as a secret commando training school. In all more than 25,000 men passed through what became known as 'The Castle', including French, Belgian and Scandinavian resistance fighters. For years afterwards those who survived the fighting continued to regard it as their spiritual home.

- **Arisaig House**, Inverness-shire. Situated outside Arisaig in Lochaber on the west coast, and now offering bed-and-breakfast, in the 1940s the house played an important role in the establishment in Scotland of the Special Operations Executive (SOE). Charged personally by Winston Churchill with 'setting Europe ablaze', some 3,000 agents of SOE – men and women – came here to learn the skills needed to carry out heroic and dangerous acts of sabotage against the Germans and German installations, and to train others to do the same sort of work in occupied countries.

- **Scotland Street Tunnel**, best known as Edinburgh's largest Second World War air-raid shelter, was actually completed nearly a hundred years earlier as part of the city's railway network. Despite the huge cost of construction the

3,000-foot-long bore was used only briefly to run trains into Canal Street (now Waverley) Station before being converted into a highly successful Victorian mushroom farm.

THE WEIRDEST THINGS FOUND IN SEWERS

In tunnels of another sort, and amidst the nearly thirty million items of sanitary waste that are flushed away every month, Scottish Water spends £7 million every year hoicking stuff out that shouldn't be there. As well as enough cooking fat to cause 20,000 blockages, the most bizarre items found in its sewers include:

A goldfish called Pooh

A Winnie the Pooh toy

A sheep

Several sets of false teeth

Deckchairs

A badger pulled unharmed from a pumping station at Drongan

One 6-foot-long Mexican Desert King Snake discovered at a waste water treatment works in Dunfermline. (Wild? It was livid.)

A cow found in a storm tank in Gatehead

Mobile phones galore, and a fax machine

One frog

An Action Man doll

An orange, apparently flushed whole down the loo

Several wedding and engagement rings

A selection of wristwatches

One traffic cone

A pink bicycle

A football

A clothes iron (still working)

A railway sleeper

A shopping trolley

And a credit card belonging to a sewage worker whose wallet had been pinched two weeks previously

- **Holy Loch,** Argyll and Bute. For decades an important base for submarines, the sea loch was the launch pad for the highly covert Operation Mincemeat. In May 1943 this spectacular exercise in enemy deception successfully planted the body of 'Major Martin' and a briefcase full of faked papers off the Spanish coast. The top-secret documents described an Allied landing in southern Europe, thereby encouraging Germany to divert troops and materiel from Sicily where the landings were actually to take place. In a high-speed overnight dash the body, actually that of a Welsh drunk, was delivered to HMS *Seraph* by the racing driver St John 'Jock' Horsfall, driving a van fitted with an Aston Martin works engine.
- **Camp 21,** Perthshire. This POW camp at Cultybraggan outside Comrie was in reality a maximum-security facility for housing many of the most fanatical Nazis to fall into British hands. These included the ringleaders of an attempted mass breakout at another camp in Wiltshire who, believing they

had been betrayed, turned on one of their own and beat him to death. The victim, Wolfgang Rosterg, was innocent (the plan was blown when the conspirators were overheard discussing the escape by a guard who spoke German) and in July 1945 eight of them were put on trial, with five being hanged for the murder at Pentonville Prison in London. At the camp itself many of the original Nissen huts have survived and are now listed as protected monuments, and the five-man hanging is on record as the 20th century's largest mass execution in Britain. The hangman Harry Allen (Britain's last) later described the five in his diary as 'the most callous men I have ever met'.

- **Camp 165,** Caithness. Located outside the village of Watten, this looked to all intents and purposes like an ordinary prisoner-of-war camp, but with its remote moorland location was another special high-security facility designed to hold so-called Black POWs. These were senior members of the Third Reich who were held for special interrogation and, where possible, re-educated as part of an organised process of de-nazification. Inmates included U-boat captain Otto Kretschmer, concentration camp commandant Paul Werner Hoppe, and SS captain and Wehrmacht propaganda chief Gunter d'Alquen. The latter was successfully 'turned' and subsequently joined the CIA to help establish an important anti-communist propaganda strategy during the Cold War. Hoppe returned to Germany and was imprisoned for war crimes after escaping execution.

- **Belhaven Hill School**, East Lothian. Situated on the coast at Dunbar, this co-educational boarding school was requisitioned as a Special Training School and codebreaking centre. Codenamed 'STS 54b' it was used to train agents as covert wireless operators before they were dropped behind enemy lines or into occupied territory. Approximately 100 graduates of the school went as so-called Jedburghs, each 'Jed' being a three-man unit – a mix of British, American, French, Dutch and Belgian officers and men – sent to support local resistance groups.

- The modern **Marine Resource Centre** on the shores of Loch Creran near Oban grew out of one of several seaweed factories producing sodium alginate fibre during the Second World War. The fibre was used to manufacture specialised military materials such as camouflage netting and artificial silk for parachutes, and there were even plans to use it to build an experimental version of the De Havilland Mosquito. The seaweed would have been used to replace some of the lightweight balsa components in the celebrated twin-engined 'wooden wonder'. Unfortunately the programme was halted in 1944, although a small portion of the miracle substance survives at the Science Museum in London.

- Shown on almost no maps, **RAF Black Isle**, about eight miles northeast of Inverness near Fortrose, was one of several 'non-airfields' used to store replacement aircraft well away from the risk of enemy action. In order not to attract attention from German overfliers these deliberately lacked all facilities usually associated with an RAF station, so that even the rough grass landing strips would have to be cleared of grazing sheep each time an aircraft needed to land or depart.

- **Royal Northern and Clyde Yacht Club** in Rhu, Argyll and Bute, provided wartime accommodation for officers from 'RAF Helensburgh', a name conceived deliberately to obscure the true function of the Marine Aircraft Experimental Establishment. Transferred from Felixstowe in Suffolk (which was felt to be uncomfortably close to Germany), the highly secretive MAEE evaluated new weapon systems, such as parachute depth charges, a Spitfire fitted with floats, and the precursor to the famous 'Dambuster' bouncing bomb. Codenamed 'Highball', the latter was tested nearby on Loch Striven using an old French Dreadnought, the *Courbet*, as a target. Always working under conditions of great secrecy, staff at MAEE were also responsible for assessing the capabilities of various captured German aircraft, including the Heinkel He-115 and an Arado Ar-196.

THE LONGEST ECHO

For decades the longest echo inside a man-made structure was believed to be the fifteen-second one at the chapel of the egocentric 10th Duke of Hamilton's family mausoleum (see the Aristocratic Scotland chapter for more on this). However, in early 2014 this was comprehensively beaten by a small team of university researchers at the Inchindown tunnels, a top-secret Second World War fuel-storage facility near Invergordon in Ross-shire.

A complex of six vast underground tunnels, each one nearly 800 feet long and containing bomb-proof tanks with walls more than a foot and a half thick, in the 1940s Inchindown was used to store up to thirty-two million gallons of furnace fuel oil for the Royal Navy. Hidden inside Kinrive Hill and last used during the Falklands War in the early 1980s, the complex is now privately owned and is only very occasionally opened to small groups of visitors. In January 2014, however, one of them, an acoustic engineer from Salford University, managed to obtain permission to have a gun fired down one of the tunnels. Loaded with blanks, it recorded an astonishing 112-second echo, a new world record.

- **Ravenscraig Hospital**, Greenock. From 1941–46 this former asylum was renamed HMCS *Niobe* and served as the UK headquarters for the Royal Canadian Navy. At the end of the war the hospital was returned to civilian use, although by the time it was handed back to the authorities all the hospital beds had disappeared. It transpired that most had been removed and welded to the hangar deck of HMS *Puncher* to provide accommodation for Canadian servicemen returning home.

- **Gruinard Island**, Ross and Cromarty. This small island halfway between Ullapool and Gairloch has been uninhabited for the last 100 years and was used for government biological weapons and germ-warfare testing during the Second World War. In 1942 this included bombing tethered sheep with anthrax to see what would happen: curiously enough all sixty of them died. The 520-acre island was afterwards quarantined for an indefinite period – forty years on nearly 400 viable spores were reportedly still present in each gram of soil – but it has since been sold back to the original owner's family for a reported £500. Ahead of this it was decontaminated by injecting nearly 3,000 tons of formaldehyde and seawater into the ground, and much of the topsoil was taken away in sealed containers.

- **An old tower on a campsite** overlooking Gallanach Road near Oban is described on some maps as simply a look-out. It is actually a 1940s minefield control tower, a three-storey concrete polygon built to guard the Sound of Kerrera at Gallenach against enemy shipping. The officer manning the tower would have been able to remotely disable or detonate mines beneath the waters of the sound once a vessel approaching the area had been identified as friendly or otherwise.

- **Montreathmont Camp Radio Station**, Angus. Situated in a clearing on Forestry Commission land in the Valley of Strathmore in central Angus, this Cold War listening post previously played a crucial role in the Second World War. As an offshoot of the famous Government Code and Cypher School – better known as Bletchley Park – the white communications block housed fifty-two code-breaking machines from the ULTRA programme used to great effect to crack the Germans' secret Enigma codes.

- **Carruthers House** on English Street in Dumfries will be known to anyone who falls into arrears with his council tax. Buried beneath the building is an armoured bunker that was completed in 1963 for the local authority for use in the event of a nuclear war. One of several in Scotland, with reinforced concrete walls and ceilings, steel blast doors, decontamination chambers, communication rooms and dormitories, this one was used for emergency meetings following the 1988 Lockerbie disaster and again during the 2001 foot and mouth crisis.

- **Kilchiaran Farm** on Islay briefly played host in the mid-1950s to a key component of NATO's airborne defences against the Soviets' nuclear-armed fleet of Tupolev Tu-4 bombers. First operational in 1949, these were reverse-engineered from the American B-29 Superfortress that dropped the Hiroshima and Nagasaki bombs, the Russians sneakily stealing both the design and technology after a number of them crash-landed in Siberia following a bombing raid on Japan. In the absence of any credible opposition from the RAF these were thought to pose a major risk, so an advanced new radar facility was installed at Kilchiaran to provide surveillance over the Atlantic coast.

- **The Guard House**, Aberdeenshire. At first glance there is not much unusual about the small stone chalet bungalow at Bervie Brow, a hill north east of Inverbervie. But once inside it is possible to descend into a vast, subterranean bunker, a space extending to more than 10,000 square feet. In the 1950s and 1960s this served as the secret command and control centre for the Inverbervie Centimetric Early Warning Radar Station. A US Navy facility designed to warn of the expected Soviet nuclear attack, it was finally shuttered in 1993.

- Screened by trees in King Duncan's Road in Inverness, an extensive Second World War-era facility known as the **Raigmore Bunker** originally comprised an ops room, a filter room and a communications centre for the Royal Observer Corps. Much modified in the years since, initially for civil defence, it now has more than sixty rooms on two levels and, situated on what has been described as 'land that cannot flood', it has been reborn as a resilient emergency control centre for Highlands Council. Its precise location is described by a council spokesman as 'discreet and yet well-known by those who need to attend it', and it is known to have its own electricity supply but also, should this fail, two bicycles rigged up to run the ventilation plant using human pedal power.

- In 1982 work began on the construction of **Royal Naval Armaments Depot (RNAD) Coulport** in Argyll, a new storage and loading facility for the Trident warheads forming part of Britain's nuclear deterrent. Sixteen heavily reinforced concrete bunkers were built into the hillside on the eastern shore of Loch Long, apparently with room for up to 100 atomic warheads held in underground vaults behind airlock doors. Beneath these are two subterranean docks to receive Vanguard nuclear submarines preparing for and returning from their routinely long patrols. Curiously, Britain owns the warheads but not the missiles to which they are fitted, which remain the property of the US government.

- **Pitrivie Castle** is a Category A-listed 17th-century house on an estate between Rosyth and Dunfermline that was once owned by the sister of Robert the Bruce. Now private apartments, until the 1990s as shore station HMS *Scotia* it was the headquarters of NATO's North Atlantic Area controlling the No. 18 Group RAF and friendly naval forces in the region. Ahead of its return to civilian use nearly all the military buildings were demolished, and a large underground bunker sealed up using explosives.

- Bizarrely, for several decades tiny **Campbeltown Airport** on the west coast of Argyll boasted Europe's longest runway, at more than 10,000 feet. Forming part of RAF Machrihanish, which in turn grew out of an old airship station, it was another important Cold War facility where the US maintained a Naval Special Warfare Detachment comprising around twenty Navy SEALS. Until 1995, when the more than 1,000-acre site was handed back to the Ministry of Defence, it was certified to receive special flights including the Space Shuttle and top secret Lockheed P-3 Orion anti-submarine and surveillance aircraft taking part in NATO exercises. Amidst rumours that the base was also used by a top secret 'Aurora' prototype capable of eight times the speed of sound, conspiracy theorists have attributed the 1994 Chinook crash in which several high-ranking intelligence officers died to an incident involving a mysterious triangular UFO.

- **Birnie House**, Perthshire. In 2007, when agents Strutt and Parker offered a large house for sale in Alyth, Blairgowrie, the unique selling points included what is thought to be Scotland's first private nuclear shelter. This had been installed in the 1960s by the owner, who was fearful of a Russian attack, at an equivalent cost today of around £250,000. However when the house went onto the market following his death his wife admitted to the press that she had been down into the 100-square-foot shelter only once, and found it frightening.

- The same year, following a massive explosion on the **Ardeer peninsula** in North Ayrshire, three small boys were reportedly helping the police with their enquiries. Nearly two dozen fire appliances were required to extinguish a serious chemical fire on a site that in the 1870s had been the first in Britain to produce Sir Alfred Nobel's new invention, 'Dynamite'. Sensibly located in an area remote from any large towns, the plant employed around 13,000 people and was the largest explosives manufacturer in the world. Today it is home to Scotland's only official mainland naturist beach.

- In 2011 one of Scotland's most mysterious tunnels came to light after being literally lost for many decades. The brick-lined tunnel was found by a gardener clearing rhododendrons from the grounds of **Falkirk's Forth Valley Royal Hospital**. It is thought to date from around 1800 and may have been excavated so that guests of the Stirling-Chalmers family at nearby Larbert House could avoid encountering any servants while walking down to the adjacent loch.

- Today **Dundrennan Range** on the Solway Firth near Kirkcudbright is the only open-air weapons testing range in the British Isles where depleted uranium weapons are permitted to be put through their paces. With several thousand DU shells said to be lying on the bed of the Firth, the range has also been used for joint MoD/US Army tests of an experimental Electro-Magnetic Launch Facility or 'rail-gun' capable of firing high-impact projectiles at speeds of 7,500 mph and over a range of more than 200 miles.

7

Island Scotland

'From the lone shieling of the misty island
Mountains divide us, and the waste of seas –
Yet still the blood is strong, the heart is Highland,
And we in dreams behold the Hebrides!'

Anon, *Blackwood's Edinburgh Magazine*,
September 1829

With around 790 of them in total, 130 of which are inhabited, Scotland's islands mostly fall into four main groups – Shetland, Orkney, and the Inner and Outer Hebrides – but others are to be found in the Clyde, Forth and Solway Firths with numerous smaller ones lapped by the fresh waters of countless lochs.

Berneray

In 1987 it was revealed that Prince Charles had visited the Sound of Harris to try for himself the simpler island life. Albeit only for a week, the Duke of Rothesay lived and worked on Berneray with a genuine crofter, planting and lifting potatoes, cutting peat, dipping sheep and planting trees. Islanders were sworn to secrecy about his stay on Donald Alex MacKillop's croft, but the duke put his experiences to use when developing his organic farm at Highgrove.

Boreray

Back in the days when St Kilda was inhabited, an annual visit would be made to Boreray each September by men from Hirta who came to hunt gannets. With no harbour and exceptionally slimy rocks at sea level, those charged with killing the birds would approach the island by boat and be dressed in stockinged feet rather than boots in order to avoid slipping over. They would then have to sneak up on the nests very quietly – gannet colonies post 'sentry' birds at night-time – before clubbing to death as many birds as possible, which would then be taken back and preserved for food.

Copinsay

A rude wake-up call for anyone who thinks the smaller, more remote islands might make a practical getaway, in 1993 a Staffordshire man bought an old lighthouse keeper's cottage on Copinsay as a holiday home, and was informed by the local power company that hooking it up to the national grid would cost him £1 million.

Eilean Kearstay

The geology of the area is such that the island carries an official Admiralty warning. Because of a strange magnetic anomaly any boats in the area relying on a traditional compass will observe that the needle sometimes strays away from north and not towards it.

Flodday

Situated south-west of Barra and so flat as to be almost washed over in a big sea, the windswept island lacks all shelter and has never been settled. Despite being something of an unpromising rock it is nevertheless the only place in the world where one can find the unique dark green butterfly *Argynnis aglaja scotica.*

Foula

These days the most remote British island to be permanently inhabited, Foula is part of Shetland but very distant from it. The thirty residents make a living from fishing and wool, and although the Scots colonised the island in the 16th century it was first settled by Norsemen around 800 years earlier and still feels decidedly Nordic.

Great Bernera

Situated at the southern end of the island, Barra Head lighthouse is the only one in Scotland to feature a Christian cross in its design. The symbol was put there in the 1830s because at the time the islanders were all Roman Catholics. Speaking no English whatsoever, and ministered to only once a year by a priest, the islanders lived in houses that, according to a visitor, 'consist of holes dug in the earth . . .with a fire of peats burning on the floor'.

Handa

Handa is sufficiently close to the Sutherland coast that centuries ago the dead would be brought to the island for burial to avoid the risk of their being dug up by wolves on the mainland. The 760-acre island was subsequently settled by a number of families who elected their oldest female 'queen' and established a kind of parliament or co-operative that met every day to decide who did which job. This democratic system reportedly worked very well until the potato famine of 1848 led everyone to seek a new life in America.

Harris

The 6th Earl of Dunmore was given the island by his father in 1834, and it was his wife who skilfully promoted the suitability of the famous tweed to dress the gamekeepers, ghillies and so forth employed by her society friends. Prior to this the cloth was woven only for the crofters themselves, but annual production subsequently soared to nearly eight million yards. Though always known as Harris Tweed, and as such an internationally protected brand, it is produced quite legally elsewhere too, including Lewis, North and South Uist, Benbecula, and Barra.

Horse Island

Briefly the subject of a mini Klondike-style goldrush, the island has long been held to be the hiding place of a hoard of Spanish gold concealed by shipwrecked Armada sailors in 1588. Three centuries later a local shepherd insisted he had found a doubloon buried in the heather, but a detailed search by several excited treasure hunters from the mainland found nothing before being called off.

Hoy

The highest spot in Orkney is also the wettest, with approximately sixty inches of rainfall a year. Hoy's celebrated Old Man, a 449-foot sea stack of old red sandstone, was first climbed in 1966 and then again when a live BBC television feed attracted an extraordinary three million viewers. The second team required several tons of equipment and included Dougal Haston, the first Scotsman to reach the summit of Mount Everest. Despite the name the Old Man is thought to be only around 250 years old, and as it is constantly assaulted by wind and water it is thought unlikely to survive much longer.

Inch Kenneth

Once owned by the celebrated Mitford family, the island provided a refuge for one of six daughters, Unity, who was severely brain-damaged by a self-inflicted shot to the head when her infatuation with Adolf Hitler failed to avert the Second World War. It was later acquired by one of her sisters, the campaigning journalist Jessica. As an ardent, life-long communist, she used to tease her siblings by saying that she might allow the Soviets to build a nuclear submarine base beneath the island.

Inchkeith

Located in the Firth of Forth, in 1493 the island became the setting for a bizarre scientific experiment. James IV, fancying himself as something of a Renaissance man, conceived a project to discover the form of the earliest human language. To test his theories he had a deaf and dumb woman transported to the island with two infants whom she was to nurse. It was hoped that when the children learned to speak, free from any normal form of human communication, they would reveal the original tongue of man. Unfortunately no one seems to have kept a record of the results, and the island was shortly afterwards used to quarantine people from Edinburgh who contracted syphilis.

Islay

The earliest sign of human habitation in Scotland was found on Islay, a flint arrowhead unearthed in a field near Bridgend. It is thought to date from around 10,800 BC and therefore predates by some 4,000 years the earliest actual human remains, which were found in a Mesolithic rubbish dump on Oronsay.

Isle of Dogs

Not strictly speaking an island, and of course not in Scotland either, this once highly industrialised corner of east London was nevertheless home to thousands of Clydesiders during the heyday of Victorian shipbuilding. As well as its own kirk it had a number of pubs such as the Burns and the Highland Mary where workers could be assured of a warm welcome and barmen who could understand their accents.

Jura

George Orwell found the island 'extremely ungetatable', but came here towards the end of his life to write *Nineteen Eighty-Four*. Almost as quiet now as it was in his day, it has a population of fewer than 200 but more than its fair share of ghosts. The only pub on the island is believed by many to be haunted, its only real road (the single-track A846) has a 'ghost car' that can be seen from time to time, and the Indian-owned whisky distillery is said to have been built in 1810 after its founder was told to do so by 'a member of the undead'. Jura is also home to the oldest stone structures found anywhere in Scotland, namely three stone hearths that are thought to date from around AD 6,000.

Kerrera

In 1249 the island was visited by Alexander II of Scotland, whose ship was anchored in Horseshoe Bay. Whilst sleeping on board the king had a dream about St Columba telling him to return home, a warning his attendants took seriously but that he felt he could ignore. Insisting they accompany him onto the island he tripped and fell the minute his foot hit dry land and was dead before he could be carried back on board.

Little Bernera

In 1962 the 250-acre island was purchased by Robin Grinnal-Milne, an eccentric Scots-born German count who also claimed to be a Yugoslavian prince. (A friend of Ian Fleming's, he may have inspired the character of Sir Hilary Bray in the 007 adventure *On Her Majesty's Secret Service.*) Decades later the count told a radio reporter that he planned to bequeath the island to Prince Harry, but on his death in 2012 there was no paperwork to support this and it quietly passed to the National Trust.

Mainland

The chief island of Orkney is home to the most malevolent of Scottish elves, the Nuckelavee, who causes epidemics among cattle and whose breath can wilt crops. Fortunately the Beane Nighe (or banshee) hails from Orkney too, a benevolent fairy who cleans the blood off people who are going to die but is ferociously ugly, with only one nostril, a single large protruding tooth, webbed toes and long hanging breasts. The island also boasts the world's oldest indoor loo, set into the wall of the Neolithic village of Skara Brae and so is conceivably more than 5,000 years old.

Mugdrum

At just 32 acres not much happens on low-lying Mugdrum or ever did, but at the Laing Museum in Newburgh there is the stuffed body of a two-headed or polycephalic kitten that was born on the island in the 1800s. (These are rare, but Eton College has another.)

North Rona

Some forty-four miles north-north east of the Butt of Lewis, this one is so remote that it is frequently left off maps of the United

Kingdom. The island was inhabited until 1685, after which the entire population died out when a shipwreck caused an infestation of black rats. These may have brought plague with them, or simply raided the community's food stores, leaving everyone to starve, and the grisly discovery was made only after another shipwreck when a group of St Kildans occupied the island for seven months. Apparently that's how long it took them to collect enough driftwood to make a boat with which to make their escape to Stornoway.

Out Stack

Probably because of its funny name Muckle Flugga is commonly held to be the northernmost point of the British Isles, but in fact the honour goes to Out Stack (or Oosta). Nearly 2,000 feet further out, it's the last bit of land before the North Pole and no more than a tiny rocky outcrop. The absence of any safe landing place almost certainly explains why in the 1850s, when it was felt necessary to build a lighthouse, Muckle Flugga was identified as the best spot. Today its staggeringly bright 910,000-candlepower beam is focused twenty-five miles out to sea by way of two hand-ground refractors.

Raasay

Long famous for having the best pipers (including Angus MacKay, the first official piper to Queen Victoria), in the 1890s the island nevertheless banned the playing of all musical instruments. This happened after its residents fell under the spell of a harsh killjoy of a man, a Free Church minister who despised all forms of physical entertainment. Twenty years later some three dozen islanders mustered under the stopped clock of Raasay House Stables before leaving for the Great War. Only a third of them returned and, as if in perpetual mourning for those lost, a hundred years later the clock still never quite functions properly.

Rum

The largest of Scotland's Small Isles (and never the smallest of the large ones), Rum was rented and then purchased by a Lancashire textile tycoon whose son and heir came here in 1897 to build on a heroic scale. George Bullough's Kinloch Castle, built of red sandstone from Dumfriesshire, required more than 300 craftsmen to complete it, including stonemasons, carpenters, woodcarvers and stained glass makers, many of them shipped in from England. More than 250,000 tons of topsoil were imported from the mainland to make a garden, and the fourteen gardeners were paid extra to wear kilts. Around the estate heated pools were provided for the owner's pet turtles and alligators, and a rare mechanical orchestrion – a device that is to an orchestra what a pianola is to a piano – piped music around the house and grounds. Once completed Bullough used it for only three weeks a year, and had his brand new mausoleum blown up and rebuilt after a visitor compared it to a public loo. Despite the luxury and self-evident expense of it all the castle was effectively thrown in for nothing when the island was sold in the 1950s for barely £1 an acre.

St Kilda

When magician Malcolm Russell (aka Parker Doodlebug) embarked on a personal magical mystery tour a few years ago he decided to stage a public performance on every one of Scotland's inhabited islands. Reaching St Kilda, he said, was by far the hardest, and he tried getting there by fishing boat, sailing boat, dive boat, Army helicopter and even a Russian icebreaker before finally making it to this most remote outpost on an exceptionally lucky daytrip.

St Ninian's Isle

This is a rare tied island, connected to the Shetland mainland by a geological feature called an active tombolo. In essence a stretch of sandy beach with water lapping it on both sides, the one at St Ninian's is the largest example in the United Kingdom and Europe's finest. The church on the island, buried for 200 years, was the scene of a remarkable discovery in 1958 when a larch-wood box was unearthed from the nave and found to contain the jawbone of a porpoise (they call them neesiks here) and an unrivalled hoard of twenty-eight priceless Pictish silver objects dating back more than a thousand years.

Shetland

From AD 872 and for more than 600 years the scattered archipelago was ruled from Scandinavia through a powerful Viking earldom. Then, in the 15th century, the islands were pledged to Scotland as part of the marriage dowry of the daughter of the King of Denmark upon her marriage to Scotland's future King James III. That pledge was never redeemed, however, so the islands stayed Scottish. Even so, more than a thousand years after the Viking longboats first set sail most of the place names here are derived from Old Norse, and a Viking longship forms part of the crest of the local RAF station at Saxa Vord in the north. (A bizarre choice for a champion of the skies, but there you go.) Interestingly, the narrow neck of Mavis Grind – the place just north of Brae where the Northmavine pen-insula joins to the rest of Shetland Mainland – is the only place on earth where it is possible to throw a stone from the North Sea into the Atlantic. Even then, you have to be good at throwing.

South Ronaldsay

One of the most spectacular discoveries in Scottish history, Orkney's Tomb of the Eagles was excavated in the 1970s by archaeologists who found 16,000 human bones from as long ago as 3100 BC. A further 725 bones were identified as belonging to the rare white-tailed sea eagle, but these were dated to much later, suggesting that the tomb had been in use by man for as much as a thousand years.

South Uist

Even weirder is the Hebridean settlement of Cladh Hallan, the only place in the British Isles where actual mummies have been found. Between 1988 and 2002 four were excavated, one of them dating from 1300 BC or about the time of King Tutankhamun. Research suggests the bodies were sunk in peatbogs first, before being retrieved months or even years later and preserved in new tombs. Even more bizarrely, two of the bodies – one female, one male – appear to have been assembled from the parts of at least six different individuals.

Tiree

Famous for its starring role in the much-loved BBC shipping forecast, in the 18th century the island was briefly the source of Tiree marble. Actually not marble at all but a species of pink flecked limestone, most of it doesn't come from Tiree now either, but is quarried in Connemara in the west of Ireland. Unusually the island has a thriving population of hares, but no rabbits.

Unst

As far north as St Petersburg and situated on the corner of the A968 and Little Hamar Road in Baltasound, Britain's best-equipped bus stop boasts curtains, a sofa, toys for the children, a TV, computer games, and even its own website: www.unstbusshelter.shetland.co.uk. The origins of this fun diversion are slightly mysterious, but the first pieces of furniture, discarded stuff made of wicker, appeared in the mid-1990s, and the shelter was carpeted shortly afterwards. Unst's nearest railway station, incidentally, is Bergen in Norway.

Whalsay

By far the best house on the island is Symbister House, a large and fine granite building completed in 1823 at a cost of £30,000. The owner was a dying man who preferred to spend his fortune rather than see it squandered by his heirs, and whilst comparisons are notoriously unreliable the cost would be equivalent today to well over £20 million. When his family took it over there was consequently no money left to maintain it, and after a few years of taking in paying guests it was converted to a school.

Wiay

About half a mile south-east of Benbecula, the 970-acre island was briefly famous as the home of a genuine grizzly bear. The island, which fortunately has been uninhabited since the Second World War, was being used to shoot an advertisement for Kleenex tissues in 1980. Hercules, its half-ton star, somehow made a break for it during filming and managed to evade his captors for more than three weeks. When he was finally brought down by a marksman with a tranquiliser gun he was found to have lost more than twenty stone. This was soon restored when the greedy animal was offered 120 pints of milk and several dozens of eggs.

8

Inventing Scotland

'Of all the small nations of this earth, perhaps only the ancient Greeks surpass the Scots in their contribution to mankind.'

Sir Winston Spencer Churchill

Tartan comes from the French *tiretain*, the kilt apparently hails from Scandinavia or maybe Ireland, Scotch eggs were invented in London in the 1730s and Anatolian Hittites were blowing into bagpipes centuries before the Scots started doing it. But even without this lot Scotland lays claim to an impressive roster of inventors and inventions, the result, it has been suggested, of its superior education system, a strong work ethic, and weather so bad that one is better off tinkering inside than wandering about doing nothing.

Communications: Moron Shall Speak unto Moron

Postcodes and pillar boxes were famously introduced by the novelist Anthony Trollope during his time as Chief Secretary to the Postmaster General, but the **world's first adhesive postage stamp** was invented by James Chalmers from Arbroath in 1838. The **postmark** was also his idea, an ingenious refinement to prevent stamps from being re-used, but somehow Englishman Sir Rowland Hill got most of the credit (and a knighthood).

Born in 1827 in Kirkcaldy, Fife, Sir Sandford Fleming was the first to propose **worldwide standardised time zones.** He also invented the concept of **the 24-hour clock** after becoming irritated at missing a train connection on a visit to Ireland because the author of the timetable had confused a.m. and p.m.

It was left to another Scotsman, Robert Wauchope of Niddrie-Marischal in Mid-Lothian, to tackle the problem of how to communicate the right time. His answer was **the time ball,** a shore-based device that from 1829 enabled ship's captains to synchronise their marine chronometers and check their accuracy while at sea. A functioning example can still be seen on top of the Nelson Monument on Calton Hill in Edinburgh, installed in 1836 for shipping in Leith harbour. Promoted to Admiral-of-the-Blue shortly before his death, Wauchope is buried in England beneath an unusual triangular headstone.

John MacCosh, who is thought to have been born in Kirkmichael in Ayrshire, took the **first ever war photographs** while serving in India as a surgeon with the Bengal Army. The earliest known examples are from the Second Sikh War of 1848, images MacCosh captured using a substantial mahogany camera. (It was, he said 'a great mistake to make things light and portable for Indian use, as if the owner himself had to carry them'.)

After zapping himself with 2,000 volts, cutting his throat with a novel rust-proof razorblade (it was glass, and broke) and being nearly crippled by a pair of bizarre inflatable shoes, failed inventor John Logie Baird finally hit paydirt with his new **television.** Described as 'seeing by wireless' and marketed as the Televisor, his new device needed a licence that cost just £2 when broadcasting began in Scotland. The Glasgow *Herald* noted that 'while some of it might not be high quality there is the consolation of the odd and unexpected, [such as] a film about liver fluke in sheep. With all that, the television owner cannot possibly regret his purchase.'

The invention of the **telephone** is generally credited to Alexander Graham Bell, the son of a pioneering Edinburgh elocutionist, but he was actually one of two inventors who filed similar patents on the same day in 1876. It took Bell a further three weeks to produce a working prototype, by which time (said his critics) it seemed to have morphed into something rather closer to his rival's design than his own. The first words spoken were, 'Mr Watson – come here – I want to see you,' which perhaps explains why Mrs Bell refused to have anything to do with it for years.

A means of printing multiple copies of a book, **stereotyping** was invented by an Edinburgh goldsmith, William Ged, in 1725. The word has now entered the language to describe an idea whose general acceptance has solidified into a thoughtless repetitiousness. (Oddly enough, cliché may have similar origins, being an onomatopoeic word representing the sound made by hot molten metal as it is poured into the stereotyper's matrix.)

Alexander Bain from Watten in Caithness devised the first ever facsimile or **fax machine.** Incredibly this was in 1846, nearly a century and a half before the technology began to dominate inter-office communications. The crofter's son was also responsible for the first ever **electric clock.**

Bored by the laborious necessities of learning and transmitting Morse code, Graham Creed's **teleprinter** was created in 1902 by modifying an old typewriter bought from a stall on Glasgow's Sauchiehall Street market.

For anyone who's ever had trouble making themselves heard in a noisy Edinburgh bar, Elaine McLuskey's invention could be just the thing. Called the **social sphere,** the Napier University student's invention is a kind of transparent cone or hood, a clear plastic helmet that encloses everything from the neck up, thereby eliminating background noise. Both parties have to wear one, and they look ridiculous, but they do seem to work.

Traffic and Transport

In one of the **earliest attempts at flight**, John Damian put on a pair of wings made from bird feathers and leapt from the battlements of Stirling Castle in a bid to impress James IV. An alchemist by training, he had earlier attempted to win favour by converting base metal into gold. When this failed he saw flight as his last chance to keep in the king's good books, and was fortunate enough to land in a dung heap, thereby escaping serious injury except to his reputation.

The modern **macadamised road** was first seen around 1820, the brainchild of an Ayrshire engineer and colliery owner called John Loudon McAdam. He was paid a measly £2,000 for an invention that swept the world, and turned down a knighthood before dying on a holiday in Dumfriesshire. The name Tarmac of course comes from adding tar to the first part of his name.

Initially used for pumping water rather than turning wheels, the world's **first practical steam engine** was invented by James Watt, a largely self-taught medical-instrument maker from Greenock. Watt's machines were more efficient, more powerful and more costly than earlier designs, and he justified the premium he charged for them by comparing their power outputs to that of a common alternative, the horse – thus paving the way for the modern concept of horsepower. He is also said to be responsible for the first screw propeller, fitted to a ship equipped with one of his engines in 1770, but a similar device had already been patented a hundred years earlier.

Replacing iron bands on wooden wheels in 1888, **pneumatic tyres**, and the astonishing comfort derived from them, made a household name of Ayrshire vet John Boyd Dunlop. His tyres won their first cycle races just a few months later (in Ireland, where he had moved to) and the Dunlop Pneumatic Tyre Co. Ltd went on to become one of Europe's largest manufacturing concerns.

For all the choppers, fixies, BMX and carbon-fibre wonders, most modern **bicycles** look not that different to the mechanically propelled, two-wheeled vehicle designed by Scottish blacksmith Kirkpatrick MacMillan in 1839. Three years later he became the first person to be charged with a **cycling traffic offence**, an 1842 newspaper report referring to a 'gentleman from Dumfriesshire bestride a velocipede of ingenious design' who was fined five bob (25p) after running down a small girl in Glasgow.

Long part of General Motors, the all-American Buick car company was founded by Arbroath expat David Dunbar Buick in 1903. The inventor of the world's first **overhead valve** or **push-rod engine**, he had one other great success with a cheap form of white enamelling for bathtubs. Even so, he died a pauper after being kicked out of the company that still bears his name.

Still with the car, Edinburgh-born George Keith Buller Elphinstone, an electrical engineer, devised a speed-recording 'accelerometer' for trains in 1909. This was quickly developed into the type of **speedometer** on which every motorist now depends.

Robert Stirling, a church minister from Methven in Perthshire, invented the **closed cycle regenerative gas engine** in 1816. At the time it failed to unseat the increasingly popular steam engine, but nearly 200 years later versions of it are under evaluation by NASA and could be used to run so-called micro-combined heat-and-power plants for a new, more eco-friendly future. (His grandfather, also a minister, invented the threshing mill.)

The Art of War

Patrick Ferguson from Pitfour in Aberdeenshire invented the **breech-loading rifle**, which was capable of maintaining a much higher rate of fire than earlier gun designs. Unfortunately, in a classic case of living by the sword, he was shortly afterwards shot and killed in South Carolina's Battle of King's Mountain in 1780.

Vice-Admiral Philip Howard Colomb (1831–99), from Knockbrex in Dumfries and Galloway, devised the first means of **communicating from one warship to another** using light signals. Based on a Morse code-type system, and revolutionary at the time, it was adopted by the Royal Navy in 1867.

Created specifically to harass enemy forces in North Africa during the Second World War, the **Special Air Service,** or **SAS**, was established by Perthshire laird Col. Sir David Stirling, and those who became the poster-boys of Britain's elite special forces. Field Marshall Montgomery personally considered him to be 'mad, quite mad', but Stirling was credited with the destruction of more than 250 enemy aircraft behind enemy lines and scores of supply dumps, before finding himself in German hands and locked up in Colditz Castle.

As the first ever commander of the Royal Flying Corps, another Scottish army officer founded its successor, the **Royal Air Force.** On April Fool's Day 1918 Lieutenant General Sir David Henderson, the son of a Clydeside shipbuilder, established this new entity as an independent body rather than a component of the Army as the RFC had been.

More bizarrely, the **United States Navy** also owes its origins to a Scotsman. It was largely the creation of John Paul Jones, a 19th-century sailor who was born on the Arbigland estate near Kirkbean in Kirkcudbrightshire, but later fled to the US after killing a fellow crew member in a dispute over money. (Funnily enough, yet another Scot, Thomas Cochrane, did the same for Chile in 1818 after being forced to leave the Royal Navy in disgrace.)

The bolt system by which the classic **Lee-Enfield rifle** is made ready to fire takes its name from the gun's inventor, Hawick-born James P. Lee. Worryingly, he built his first gun before his thirteenth birthday. That one didn't fire well if at all but, once perfected, the Lee-Enfield remained in service with the British Army for the next sixty-three years.

Curiously, another equally significant advance in military ordnance – the **percussion cap** – was invented by an Aberdonian clergyman. A keen amateur wildfowler, Alexander John Forsyth (1768–1843) was offered £20,000 to defect to France with his device, but fortunately declined to side with Napoleon.

Portable camouflage, in the form of the military **Ghillie Suit**, was first used during the Second Boer War (1899–1902) by a Scottish Highland yeomanry regiment, the Lovat Scouts. The unit also provided the British Army with its first official trained **snipers**.

Working mostly in Suffolk, but born in Brechin in Angus, Robert Watson-Watt was a meteorologist who is today remembered for his success in perfecting the technology behind **radar**. His employers had been hoping for some kind of radio-powered 'death ray', but when Watson-Watt demonstrated how he could locate a Supermarine Scapa flying boat nearly twenty miles out at sea the value of radar – aka Radio Detection And Ranging – was immediately obvious. Incidentally, much the same technology is used in **microwave ovens**.

Both the **Bank of England** and the **Bank of France** have Scottish origins. The establishment of the first of these, now notable among many things for its famous three-foot-long vault keys, was proposed by William Paterson in 1691. A banker from Tinwald in Dumfriesshire, he saw it as an efficient way to pay for an expensive war with France. Across the Channel, where he was Louis XV's Controller General of Finances, John Law from Fife established something similar, as well as suggesting that coins should be ditched in favour of paper money.

In 1728 the Royal Bank of Scotland authorised the **world's first overdraft**, although in the light of the bank's subsequent behaviour this may no longer be regarded as such an achievement.

In 1965 Paisley-born engineer James Goodfellow devised a machine that allowed bank customers to access their money outside normal working hours. This was the first **automatic telling machine** or cashpoint, and the first one in Britain was installed in a branch of Barclays Bank in Enfield, north London. The **PIN** or personal identity number was also his idea, and the first customer to use it was *On the Buses* actor Reg Varney.

Publishing

Assumed to be English but American for well over a century, *Encyclopaedia Britannica* was first published in 1768 in Edinburgh by Colin Macfarquhar and Andrew Bell. Since then its contributing authors have included more than 100 Nobel laureates and at least five US presidents.

The American business magazine *Forbes* is named for its founder Bertie Charles Forbes (1880–1954), who was born in New Deer, Aberdeenshire. He worked as a local newspaper journalist before seeking his fortune in South Africa and New York, and after spending the bulk of his professional career in the US chose to be buried near his birthplace beneath the Hill of Culsh.

In 1835 another Scot, James Gordon Bennett, founded the *New York Herald*. Born in New Mills in Banffshire, he conducted the **world's first newspaper interview** (as part of a shocking front-page exclusive about the murder of a prostitute) and was also the first journalist to be granted an exclusive audience with an American president.

The first ever **permanent colour photograph** was taken and developed by James Clark Maxwell in 1861, and was of a tartan ribbon. Born in India Street, Edinburgh – there is a statue of him on George Street – Clark Maxwell also discovered the relationship between electricity, magnetism and light, but was nevertheless nick-named 'Daftie' by his chums in the Royal Scottish Academy. Unlike all of them, however, he has the unusual distinction of having an entire mountain range named after him – even if it is on Venus.

The *Dandy* was first published by DC Thomson in Dundee in 1937 and six years later, in a strip called 'The Amazing Mr X', the company created the first **all-British super-hero**.

Science and Medicine

An Ayrshire farmer's son who served on the Western Front during the Great War, Alexander Fleming's fame depends on his accidental discovery of penicillin, the world's first medical **antibiotic**. For this he was knighted by George VI, and in Madrid grateful matadors erected a statue of him because so many of them would otherwise have died of wounds received during the course of their work.

Born in Cupar, Fife, the inventor of the **hypodermic syringe** was Alexander Wood (1817–84). His wife is popularly supposed to have been the first drug addict to die as a result of an accidentally injected overdose, but in fact she outlived him by many years and died of natural causes.

Now largely forgotten, the Gregorian telescope was the **first ever reflecting telescope**. It was designed by the Aberdeenshire mathematician and astronomer James Gregory in the mid-17th century and pre-dates the first Newtonian telescope, built by Sir Isaac Newton in 1668. Its creator lost out, however, because it was another five years before anyone studied Gregory's design and built a working prototype.

Unsurprisingly, James Young Simpson's discovery that chloroform was the first truly **practical general anaesthetic** proved so popular with long-suffering patients that when he died in

1870 Scotland declared a national holiday. More than 100,000 people lined the streets to see his funeral cortege pass through Edinburgh.

The first house to be lit by gas was in Cornwall, but it belonged to a Scot. William Murdoch (1754–1839) was born at Lugar in Ayrshire and, while most famous as the Scot who lit the world, he also devised a steam tricycle, a steam-powered cannon and the **world's first waterproof paint**.

The use of **ultrasound scanners** for medical diagnosis was introduced in the 1950s by Ian Donald, a professor of midwifery at Glasgow University. He got the idea after learning that similar technology was used to check for flaws in the metal used in the city's shipyards.

Born at Merchiston Castle outside Edinburgh, the 16th-century mathematician John Napier had five sons and five daughters but nevertheless found the time, space and peace to invent **logarithms**. These, he boasted, 'doth clean take away all the difficulty that heretofore hath been in mathematical calculations'. As the 8th Laird of Merchiston he also invented **the decimal point** and a device called Napier's Bones, a type of Occidental abacus. Curiously, for an authentic man of science, his hobbies included alchemy, witchcraft and collecting books that proved the Pope was the Antichrist.

A medical missionary from Beith in Ayrshire, Henry Faulds invented the science of **forensic fingerprinting** in 1880. He did this after going on an archaeological dig in Japan and noticing how the imprints of long-dead craftsmen could be discerned on the fragments of pottery being unearthed. Studying his own fingertips when he got home, and those of friends, he quickly realised that the patterns were unique.

Any Other Business

Described as an eccentric Orkney genius, Davie Taylor was an ageing crofter from Firth who in 1891 bodged up a 'bib and brace sort of clasp for hooking his breeks up'. Five years later teenager Andrew Thomson, an apprentice draper from Stromness, modified the clasp to secure ladies' stockings before obtaining a patent for what we would now recognise as **the world's first set of suspenders**.

Although he was not known for wearing a distinctive pointy hat (or standing in corners for that matter), **the world's first dunce** was the 13th-century Scottish theologian John Duns Scotus. He was widely ridiculed by humanists, who coined his name as a means of describing an idiot.

Thomas Crapper has somehow stolen the credit, but the Edinburgh watchmaker and mechanic Alexander Cummings was the first to patent a design for a **flushing lavatory**. In 1775 he also invented the s-trap or u-bend we rely on today, in which standing water prevents nasty niffs backing up from the sewer or cesspit down below.

Born in Jedburgh, Roxburghshire in the 1780s, Sir David Brewster developed an interest in optics that led him in 1817 to build the **first ever kaleidoscope**. The name came from the ancient Greek *kalos* (beautiful), *eidos* (something that is seen) and *skopeo* (to examine) but its inventor neglected to patent his idea in time. As a result he made little or no money from it, despite selling hundreds of thousands in the first three months of manufacture.

The Kincardine chemist and physicist James Dewar made a similar mistake when he invented **the vacuum flask** in 1892, probably because he was thinking of using it for lab work rather than on picnics. As well as not profiting from his ingenuity, he missed his only chance at immortality. With millions still in use today, everyone calls his invention the Thermos and never, ever the Dewar.

Pianoforte is Italian for soft-strong, but it was an East Lothian carpenter called John Broadwood who developed the idea of using a **foot-pedal for varying the sound** of the instrument.

Broadwood also revolutionised the instrument's boxy design, which was based on that of old-fashioned clavichords and spinets, and after building **the world's first grand piano** in 1777 sold examples of it to Mozart, Chopin and Beethoven.

The original macintosh, in those days a coat not a computer, was sold in 1824. It was named after the Glaswegian inventor Charles Macintosh, who created **one of the first waterproof fabrics** by rubberising sheets of material in his textile factory.

A Scot working for General Electric during the Second World War, in 1943 James Wright dropped boric acid into silicone oil and discovered that the resulting goo stretched further and bounced higher than existing kinds of rubber. The result, which the company nicknamed **nutty putty**, seemed to lack any military applications, so they sold the idea for $147. As Silly Putty or Potty Putty it has been a Christmas bestseller ever since.

9

Aristocratic Scotland

Our Duiks were deills, our Marquesses were mad,
Our Earls were evil, our Viscounts yet more bad,
Our Lords were villains, and our Barons knaves
Who wish our burrows did sell us for slaves.
They sold the church, they sold the State and Nation,
They sold their honour, name and reputation,
They sold their birthright, peerages and places
And now they leave the House with angrie faces.

Anon, *Verses on the Scots Peers* (1706)

For the philosopher and statesman Edmund Burke, nobility was 'a graceful ornament to the civil order . . . the Corinthian capital of polished society'. But he was Irish, and for many the best that can be said for Scotland's titled class is that they're every bit as eccentric as the English.

- In 1712 the **4th Duke of Hamilton** – remembered as 'a bone-headed wastrel' – challenged the 4th Baron Mohun to a duel. After running him through with a sword he was in turn killed by Lord Mohun's second, who was then set upon by the duke's man. Within minutes the two noblemen were dead, and with two more grievously injured the scene was reportedly so bloody that the government was persuaded immediately to ban duels using swords. Thereafter only pistols would be permitted, apparently in the belief that this would result in less horrific injuries.

- The explorer **James Bruce of Kinnaird** made such outlandish claims in his *Travels to Discover the Source of the Nile*, published in 1790, including a description of attending an Abyssinian feast at which those attending cut raw steaks from live oxen, that Dr Johnson, admittedly no friend of the Scots, publicly doubted whether he had even set foot in the country. (Johnson, it may be recalled, thought Scotland 'a vile country'.)

- The founding president of London's smart new Royal Automobile Club in 1897, the **4th Duke of Sutherland** owned four Rolls-Royces and insisted the engine in at least one of them be kept running at all times to be ready for an immediate departure should he decide it was required.

- In marked contrast to the familiar picture of vast and desolate estates of mountain, loch and wild grouse moor, a leading Scottish peeress, **Mary Elizabeth Temple-Nugent-Brydges-Chandos-Grenville, 11th Lady Kinloss** (1852–1944), owned much of Old Nichol, a notorious slum in the East End of London. An authentically Dickensian vision of degradation and horror, this was swept away in 1892 and replaced by Britain's first council estate. Her ladyship's role in what had become known as 'the sweater's hell' only came to light at this point, when she demanded her lawyers seek compensation for her loss of rental income.

- The first peer ever to suffer the humiliation of being temporarily expelled from the House of Lords was **Francis Douglas Stuart, 18th Earl of Moray**, in 1937, after being seen to roll a cigarette during a debate on divorce.

- In 1947, when the **Duke of Buccleuch** moved back into one of his three ancestral seats (the house had been requisitioned for the duration of the war as a possible repository for treasures removed from the British Museum), it was noted that he had no fewer than fourteen paintings by Van Dyck in his personal lavatory.

- In the 1920s, long before it was fashionable, **Nina Benita, wife of the 13th Duke of Hamilton**, was giving vegetarian dinners and telling guests, 'Not only do I cordially dislike the taste, but I believe it to be unhygienic to eat any animal flesh.' She later founded the Animal Defence and Anti-Vivisection Society, but at the time was regarded as something of a crank.

- As early as 1931 the beautiful socialite **Margaret Whigham**, later to marry the 11th Duke of Argyll, whom she met on a train in France, was spotted at a ball wearing luminous nail varnish.

- Her granddaughter and heiress Mary Freeman-Grenville was also a direct descendent of the sister of the tragic 'Nine Days Queen' Lady Jane Grey. This made the **12th Lady Kinloss** a legitimate Tudor claimant to the throne of England, but on being told this in 1968 she insisted, 'I wouldn't take the job for all the tea in China. I have quite enough to do looking after a family of three.'

- Arriving in Aberdeen accompanied by his favourite wolfhound, in July 1922 the **Duke of Leinster** won a massive wager by completing the journey by Rolls-Royce from London in just over fourteen hours. He pocketed £3,000 for the feat – nearly half a million today – but, always impoverished, he died in the London bedsit where he worked as a caretaker.

- In 1952 **Dr Elizabeth Forbes-Sempill**, daughter of the 18th Lord Sempill of Craigievar Castle, caused a sensation by changing her name to Ewan and marrying her housekeeper. The implied change in sex was highly contentious but, working as a GP in Aberdeenshire, Dr Forbes-Sempill was subsequently able to succeed to the Forbes of Craigievar baronetcy, which had hitherto passed only down the male line.

- **Lucy Houston** (1857–1936) was a warehouseman's daughter and proselytising nudist who married well, several times. Her third marriage was to 'a hard, ruthless, unpleasant bachelor', an industrialist from Renfrewshire. When he died, Sir Robert Houston Bt left her £5.5 million, an earlier version of the will (in which she was left only £1 million) having been torn up by a furious Lucy. Much of the money she spent disseminating some of her ugly neo-fascist ideas, but she later redeemed herself by funding early work on the aircraft that was subsequently developed into the war-winning Supermarine Spitfire.

- The **10th Duke of Argyll** disliked everything modern, particularly the telephone and the motor car, and in the 1940s could be seen greeting tourists arriving at Inveraray Castle by singing famous arias from Italian operas to them. The scene was comic but also rather sad, and in 1944 the seventy-two-year-old pleaded guilty at Dunoon Sheriff's Court to assaulting a seventy-nine-year-old. In fact His Grace had long suspected that he was actually mad rather than merely eccentric, and courageously refused to marry or sire an heir in order to prevent the transmission of any rogue genes.

- No Scotsman, admittedly, but there is a memorial to **Lord Kitchener** at Marwick Head in Orkney as he was killed here in the tragic sinking of the HMS *Hampshire* off Birsay in 1916. Prior to this he had ordered his Rolls-Royce to be painted bright yellow so that policemen could see him coming and keep the rest of the traffic out of his way.

- In 2011 it was revealed that the **3rd Baron Glenconner** (1926–2010), an eccentric millionaire with his own island in the Caribbean as well as a 5,000-acre estate and a castle in Peebleshire, had named none of the members of his family in his will. Instead leaving millions of pounds' worth of property to a favourite manservant called Kent Adonai.

- Whilst he has never made the claim himself, the present and **10th Duke of Buccleuch** is another significant pretender to the throne of England, as a direct descendent of Charles II's first-born son, the Duke of Monmouth. The king always denied that he was married to Lucy Walter, Monmouth's mother, but this was widely disbelieved at the time. Today it is still disputed in some quarters, in particular by those who would prefer to see a King Richard IV on the throne than a Queen Elizabeth II.

- The **1st Lord Kelvin**, son of a Glasgow University mathematics professor, was the first person to propose marriage by undersea telegraph. In 1874, while engaged in laying 2,500 miles of cable across the Atlantic, the pioneering physicist sent a signal, 'Will you marry me?' and received one by return reading, 'Yes,' from his future wife, Fanny Blandy, who lived on the island of Madeira.

NINE LORDS A-LEAPING:
SCOTTISH DUKES IN ORDER OF SENIORITY

The Duke of Rothesay (1398)

Also known as the Prince of Wales, who also holds the title of Earl of Carrick. The first was David Stewart, son of Robert III of Scotland, although the title dropped out of use in the early 1600s until it was revived at the request of Queen Victoria.

The Duke of Hamilton (1643)

Scotland's premier peer is also the Duke of Brandon (see below). As the Hereditary Keeper of the Palace of Holyrood House, the official royal residence in Scotland, in 1999 the present holder – a bastion of inherited privilege – was permitted to carry the crown at the inauguration of that seat of modern democratic power, the new Scottish Parliament. The duke's ancestral seat, Hamilton Palace, alas, is long gone, undermined – literally – by the source of his family's wealth, which was coal. Subsidence from all the workings under the estate led to its demolition in the 1920s.

The Duke of Buccleuch (1663)

As well as seventeen titles Britain's largest private land-owner now has around 240,000 acres, well down on his 1872 ancestor at 460,000 (plus some more in England), and not even close to the aforementioned 4th Duke of Sutherland, who still holds the all-time record of around 1,358,000 acres in 1900. But even with nearly a quarter of a million acres to call his own, he is nevertheless far from being the richest duke. Most of the land is highly rural and relatively unproductive, and thus no match for the rival ducal estates that were profitably developed in and around central London by the Dukes of Westminster, Bedford, Norfolk and Northumberland.

The Duke of Lennox (1675)

A title most recently created for an illegitimate son of Charles II, the present duke holds three other dukedoms: of Richmond, of Gordon and of Aubigny-sur-Nère in France. Although Lennox is a Scottish title, originally bestowed on the head of the Clan Stewart of Darnley, the ancestral seat is Goodwood House in West Sussex. Freddie, the present duke's grandfather, is the only duke ever to win a motor race at Brooklands.

The Duke of Argyll (1701)

Tracing their origins to Sir Colin of Lochow, who was knighted in 1280, the family is thus related to Jenny von Westphalen (1814–81), who married Karl Marx and, whilst living in poverty in London's Soho, produced four daughters all of whom were called Jenny. In 1950 the 11th Duke spent a small fortune searching in vain for Spanish gold presumed to have been lost off the coast of Tobermory in the wreck of an Armada galleon that had come to grief 360 years before.

The Duke of Atholl (1703)

The Atholl family played a major role in the infamous Highland Clearances, and their trustees are still massive landowners, although the Atholls long ago surrendered one of several subsidiary titles that gave them absolute sovereignty over the Isle of Man. This lasted until 1765 when the British government acquired the rights to the island for £70,000, making the ruling sovereign the Lord of Man, although the queen never uses this title herself.

The Duke of Montrose (1707)

Reportedly weighing more than 11 lb at birth, the 7th Duke, who died in 1992, saw his Scottish estates dwindle from 130,000 acres to about 10,000 before striking out for southern Africa. Settling in Rhodesia, he was one of the signatories to that country's Unilateral Declaration of Independence, but escaped prosecution under the 14th-century Treason Act, which had been used justify the executions of two Irishman: Roger Casement during the First World War and William Joyce (Lord Haw-Haw) after the Second.

The Duke of Roxburghe (1707)

Uniquely, from 1805–12, the dukedom lay dormant as four different claimants jostled for position following the death of the 4th Duke. To resolve the issue, the House of Lords spent seven years poring over literally millions of words of genealogical opinion and evidence before deciding who might succeed as the 5th. Unfortunately the legal process was so expensive that when one of the four, Sir James Innes, was declared the winner almost his first act was to sell off the family silver. In particular this meant the exceptionally valuable collection of books amassed by the 3rd Duke, a sad, lonely but immensely knowledgeable bibliophile. His library was at this time considered to be the finest in private hands in Britain, and 200 years later the members of the highly exclusive Roxburghe Club still meet to celebrate and perpetuate the production of outstandingly beautiful and worthy tomes. At any one time there are never more than forty members, and of those past and present twenty-eight have been dukes.

The Duke of Fife (1900)

The last non-royal dukedom was conferred on the 6th Earl of Fife by Queen Victoria when he married Princess Louise of Wales, daughter of the future King Edward VII. The present duke lives on his Elsick House estate near Stonehaven in Kincardineshire, and although his position was once possibly nearly usurped (by Sir Winston Churchill, who is thought to have turned down the chance to become the Duke of Dover) it seems highly unlikely now that a sovereign will ever again create a new dukedom of this sort.

And One Distinctive Extinction: The Duke of Berwick (1687)

The illegitimate son of James II, the 1st and last Duke of Berwick blotted his copybook early on by joining the French Army. Rising to the rank of Marshal of France, and playing a leading role in some thirty campaigns, he found himself opposing his uncle the 1st Duke of Marlborough before his head was removed by a lucky shot from a cannon at the Siege of Philippsburg.

Scotland's Proudest Man: The 10th Duke of Hamilton (1767–1852)

With two ducal titles, a couple of marquessates, the earldoms of Angus, Arran, Cambridge and Lanark, and the baronies of (deep breath) Abernathy, Jedburgh Forest, Polmont, Machanshire, Aven, Innerdale and Dutton, it is little wonder that Alexander Hamilton was a big head.

His contemporaries described him as the proudest man of his day, and more sarcastically as *Magnifico*, especially once he let it be known that (in his opinion, at least) he was the rightful king of Scotland. He claimed descent through an earlier earl of Arran, but unfortunately so did his near-contemporary John James Hamilton, Marquess of Abercorn, who, it should be said, had the stronger claim. The two men also argued over who was the rightful Duc de Chatelherault, and when he lost, our man constructed an immense folly on his estate, calling it the 'Chateau de Chatelherault' in a bid to reinforce the lie.

Among his other interests Hamilton was fascinated by ancient Egyptian mummies, and the techniques used to send their owners into the afterlife. So fascinated that he contacted an acknowledged expert in the field after spending an astonishing £11,000 obtaining a vast stone sarcophagus and hauling it back from Thebes. The expert, Thomas Pettigrew, was instructed to preserve Hamilton's body when the time came, and to inter it in the aforesaid sarcophagus.

Unfortunately, for all this money (equivalent today to approximately £6 million) His Grace had acquired a sarcophagus intended for someone a good deal smaller than himself. He assumed she was a princess, though it is more likely to have been made for a minor courtier, but either way the upshot was that he couldn't fit inside it and the stone was too hard to allow for any modifications.

Distraught at the waste of money, Hamilton eventually turned his attention to the construction of a huge new mausoleum. Beneath a dome some 120 feet high were installed copies of Ghiberti's baptistry doors from Florence, an ornate octagonal family chapel, marble floors inlaid with semi-precious stones – some 10,000 pieces from forty-two Italian quarries – statues galore, and niches for his nine predecessors and all future 'heirs' to the throne of Scotland.

'What a grand sight it will be', he liked to tell visitors, 'when Twelve Great Dukes of Hamilton all rise together here at the Resurrection.' But even this idea couldn't take his mind off the problem of his coffin. Hamilton continued to worry over it, and on his deathbed his last gasp was said to be, 'Double me up! Double me up!' Sadly this proved impossible, and in the end the family took the bizarre decision to amputate his feet before having the eager Pettigrew go to work in accordance with His Grace's wishes.

It was a grim end for anyone, let alone Britain's proudest man, and sadly at a cost of £130,000 the mausoleum fared little better, taking another five years to complete even once its intended occupant was dead. On the plus side it's still there, although the immense weight of all that stone has caused it to sink by more than twenty feet, although despite having underfloor heating the chapel has never been used for a service. Unfortunately, with its astonishing fifteen-second echo the congregation could never hear what was going on and so chose to worship elsewhere. For years this echo was thought to be the world's longest in a man-made structure, but in January 2014 a resounding 112-second one was recorded in the Inchindown Tunnels near Invergordon. (More on this in the Secret Scotland chapter.)

Peerless Peers

When the Glorious Revolution removed King James II and VII from the thrones of England, Ireland and Scotland, the fugitive monarch continued to create new peers, in the belief that he retained the right. His successors kept the habit, and in Jacobite circles the titles certainly had some cachet, although they were never recognised in British law. Several are still current (see below) but rarely if ever used by the title holders.

Duke of Melfort	1692–1902
Duke of Perth	1701–1902
Duke of Mar	1715 to date
Duke of Rannoch	1717 to date
Duke of St Andrews	1717 to date
Duke of Inverness	1727–40
Duke of Fraser	1740–1815
Duchess of Albany	1783–89
Marquess of Seaforth	1690–1815
Marquess of Forth	1692–1902
Marquess of Drummond	1701–1902
Marquess of Kenmure	1707 to date
Marquess of Stirling	1715 to date
Marquess of Blair	1717 to date
Marquess of Borland	1717 to date
Marquess of Beaufort	1740–1815

LONDON'S MOST EXCLUSVE LUNCHEON CLUB

In late 2009 James Graham, the 8th Duke of Montrose, and Torquhil Campbell, the 18th Duke of Argyll, joined eight of their peers* for oysters and Dover sole at Wilton's in St James's. They were guests of the society magazine *Tatler*, which was celebrating its tercentenary. Although fourteen other dukes declined the invitation, following this rare decaducal gathering – almost certainly one not equalled since the coronation more than half a century earlier – it was calculated that between them the ten men represented the accumulation of 'some 340,000 acres, more than £2 billion and 4,505 years of aristocratic moving and shaking'. Not bad, particularly as some of the richer and longer established invitees chose to stay away.

* The Dukes of Rutland, Somerset, Northumberland, Bedford, Norfolk, Leinster, St Albans and Wellington.

Landowners Then and Now

SCOTLAND'S TOP TEN TERRITORIAL MAGNATES 1872 . . .

The Duke of Sutherland	1,358,545 acres
The Duke of Buccleuch	460,108 acres
The Earl of Breadalbane	438,358 acres
Lady Matheson	424,560 acres
Sir Charles Ross	356,500 acres
The Earl of Seafield	305,930 acres
The Earl of Fife	249,220 acres
Sir Alexander Matheson	220,663 acres
The Duke of Atholl	201,640 acres
Lord Lovat	181,791 acres

According to the maths, at this time these nine men and one woman between them owned more than a fifth of Scotland's total landmass. (By comparison the ten largest landowners in England controlled less than 2% of the total.)

... AND NOW?

The Forestry Commission	1,600,000 acres
The Scottish Executive	260,000 acres
The Duke of Buccleuch	240,000 acres
National Trust for Scotland	175,000 acres
Alcan Highlands	135,000 acres
Duke of Atholl Charitable Trust	130,000 acres
Capt. Alwyn Farquharson	125,000 acres
The Duke of Westminster	120,000 acres
The Earl of Seafield	105,000 acres
Crown Estate	100,000 acres

Despite the intrusion of public, trust and charitable bodies, and several foreign owners the precise size of whose holdings cannot readily be quantified, it is still estimated that more than half of Scotland's private land is controlled by a mere 432 families. Such a concentration is unparalleled in the developed world.

Inherited Power of Another Kind

The most powerful passenger steam locomotives ever built to run in Britain were the 3,300-horsepower London Midland and

Scottish Railway Coronation Class engines. Initially painted Caledonian Railway blue with silver banding (to match the Coronation Scot trains they were built to haul), they were called Big Lizzies by railwaymen at the time. These days they are more commonly known as Duchesses, as individual engines were named after the duchesses of Hamilton, Montrose and Sutherland. The first of these, its striking 1938 Art Deco streamlining now a symphony in crimson, is preserved at the National Railway Museum in York, a reminder not just of the great days of steam but of a time when Scotland's aristocracy really was a power in the land.

10

Building Scotland

'ar-chi-tect \är-ke-,tekt\ n. One who believes that conception comes before erection.'

Anon

From its oldest building to one of the newest – that is, from Orkney's 5,700-year-old Knap of Howar to the opinion-dividing, Spanish-designed Scottish Parliament – Scotland's single-minded approach to architecture has left us a legacy that includes some of the strangest buildings in the British Isles.

1178: The foundation of **Arbroath Abbey**, once the richest in Scotland. In ruins by 1590 – much of the stone was pinched to build the neighbouring town – it hit the headlines again in 1951 when the celebrated Stone of Scone was found on the altar. This had been stolen from Westminster Abbey on Christmas Day the year before, a crime the Dean of Westminster described as 'senseless' and that led to the English-Scottish border being closed for the first time in more than 400 years.

1297: Beneath the ruins of Yester Castle, outside the village of Gifford in East Lothian, the **Goblin Ha'** is a large vaulted subterranean hall nearly 40 feet long and 13 feet wide. Large by the standards of medieval undercrofts, it is said to be where Sir Hugo de Giffard – a powerful Scottish warlock and necromancer – used to practise his sorcery. More seriously, the vaulting is a unique and very early example of secular gothic arch-building north of the border.

1358: Rebuilt after a catastrophic fire, **St Giles Cathedral** or the **High Kirk of Edinburgh** contains two nice Scottish touches. As well as a bagpiping angel carved into the entrance arch to one of the chapels, there is a plaque commemorating the popular local heroine Jenny Geddes. She was a local market stall-holder who hurled a stool at a preacher in 1637 because he was reading from an English prayer book.

1385: In a similar vein, at the Cistercian **Melrose Abbey** in the Borders, a gargoyle depicts the earliest known representation – possibly the only representation – of a pig playing the bagpipes. Though carved from stone they are also thought to be the oldest bagpipes anywhere in Scotland.

1471: A rare Scottish almshouse, **Provand's Lordship** in Castle Street is also the oldest house in Glasgow. It was originally built for the chaplain to the (long vanished) Hospital of St Nicholas, but was later used by the lord or master of the Prebend of Barlanark – hence the name – and today it houses a museum of religious life and art.

1560: The largely self-explanatory **Repentance Tower** at Ecclefechan in Stirlingshire was built above its lonely graveyard by one John Maxwell. It was constructed as a penance for Maxwell's betrayal of a dozen of his countrymen to the English

– all of whom were promptly executed – but unfortunately he obtained the building materials by demolishing a nearby chapel, somewhat diminishing the gesture.

1576: A **fortified doocot** (or dovecote) at Mertoun in Roxburghshire bears witness to the value of these useful birds, as both meat and medicine. The Normans barred anyone but the church and prominent landowners from keeping them, and a 17th-century pharmacopoeia was one of many to recommend 'a live pigeon cut along the backbone and clapt hot upon the head' as a cure for depression. Another offered 'the powder of the dung of pigeons' as an alternative, and with such delights in mind landowners frequently tried to tempt the birds from their neighbours' estates, a favourite bait being boiled thistle-root mashed with herring.

1685: Britain's own black hole of Calcutta, **Dunnottar Castle** near Stonehaven was ruined during the Civil War. Years later the dungeons were used to hold 167 Covenanters – including forty-five women – for refusing to accept the religious authority of the sovereign.

1742: Sir John Clerk of Penicuik excavated the **Hurley Grotto**, a 130-foot-long tunnel with a fortified entrance of military appearance and bearing the inscription *TENNEBROSA OCCULTAQUE CAVE* (Beware of Dark and Secret Things). Clerk himself considered it 'a frightful cave', and admitted that some of his visitors 'stand in doubt as to whether they are among the living or the dead'. It was nevertheless no mere subterranean chamber of horrors, Clerk insisting it was built as a scientific instrument, namely a new sort of telescope. By standing at one end a knowledgeable man of science could accurately determine the sun's diameter, or at least that was the idea.

1745: At **Traquair House** in the Borders the gates – known as the Bear Gates – are the main point of interest. These are supposed to have been chained closed ever since Bonnie Prince Charlie passed through them after the Battle of Culloden. According to local legend the Earl of Traquair decided that no one should use them until a Stuart king was back on the throne. Displayed in the house itself are the cradle in which Mary, Queen of Scots, rocked the future James VI, and a sort of 16th-century portable calculator made of bone.

1748: Construction work began on **Fort George** on the Moray Firth. One of the great achievements of military engineering, it is still in military occupation nearly 250 years after its completion. Now the new garrison of the Black Watch, 3rd Battalion, Royal Regiment of Scotland, it is a remarkable thought that in all that time its armaments have never once been fired in anger.

1761: Scotland's most extraordinary holiday home, **the Pineapple** at Dunmore Park in Stirlingshire is a superbly detailed carved-stone replica of the fruit more than fifty feet high and with two small bedrooms in the wings. Built for the 4th Earl of Dunmore and beautifully restored in the mid-1970s, it is popularly supposed to commemorate the first example of the tropical delicacy to be grown in Scotland, although this almost certainly occurred elsewhere and several decades earlier.

1766: The strangely named **Arthur's O'on** (or oven) at Penicuik House in Mid Lothian is actually a dovecote. It is also a replica of a Roman temple of victory that stood by the Antonine Wall in Stirlingshire until, scandalously, this was pulled down in 1735. Its replacement was built by the son of the aforementioned Sir John Clerk, and according to tradition no rent is paid to the Crown for the land on which it is built, providing the local laird stands on the Buck Stane – an obelisk in Braid Road, Edinburgh – and blows three blasts on a horn whenever the sovereign is hunting nearby.

1768: When the four Scottish Adam brothers – John, Robert, James and William – took a ninety-nine-year lease on a substantial plot of riverside land in central London they called their result-ing development **Adelphi** from *Adelphoi*, the Greek for brothers. Modelling their buildings on the Emperor Diocletian's ruined palace at Split in Dalmatia – and creating London's first large speculative development – they relied on cheap labour to build it by importing workers from Scotland and employing pipers to keep them happy.

1778: At Mellerstain near Kelso the **Hundy Mundy** is the work of the aforementioned Robert Adam, an intriguing eye-catcher designed to be seen from the nearby country house of the Hon. George Baillie. The origin of the name is unknown but in 1933, when the 12th Earl of Haddington rode in the Grand National, as a descendent of Baillie he named his horse Handy Mundy.

1789: As its late date suggests, **Hume Castle** is a fake, built 600 feet above Greenlaw in the Borders as a picturesque ruin. It was constructed on top of genuine fortifications, however, the remains of a castle that was slighted by the despised Oliver Cromwell and blown up in 1651. What we see today, then, is little more than a landscape ornament, the creation of the 3rd Lord Marchmont, who bought the land on which it stands in 1770. Militarily it has proved its worth only once, sort of, when it was used as a look-out in 1804. From this vantage point a foolish sergeant in the Berwickshire Volunteers thought he saw something and called out 3,000 troops to repel a Napoleonic invasion force that never materialised.

1806: **Megginch Castle**, a vaguely Chinese-Gothick folly in Perthshire, was built by Captain Robert Drummond of the East India Company. His ship, the *General Elliot*, was the first in the fleet to be copper-bottomed, and is represented in miniature by the weathervane above the stableyard.

1806: With ninety-seven steps to the top the **Nelson Monument** at Forres commemorates Britain's greatest sea-faring hero, and was completed within months of his death. Unlike the more famous one in London, that is, where it took thirty-two years just to form a committee to discuss the idea and a further three decades to get the job done.

1807: **Rosetta House**, a manor on the outskirts of Peebles, owes its name to the original owner, Dr Thomas Young, who was a famous polymath and keen Egyptologist. Skilled if not quite fluent in Hebrew, Aramaic, Chaldean, Syriac, Samaritan, Arabic, Greek, Latin and Persian (not to mention Italian, French, German and Turkish), he offered 'original and insightful innovations' that helped to decipher the famous Rosetta Stone once this had been liberated from the French Army.

1811: Situated eleven miles offshore from Arbroath, **Bell Rock** is the world's oldest surviving rock or sea-washed lighthouse. Built using 2,835 pieces of three different stones quarried at Aberdeen, Edinburgh and Dundee, and 100 feet high, the ingenious construction is of such high quality that it has never been replaced. The original warning to mariners came from two clockwork bells that sounded every half-minute, hence the name, but the job is now done more conventionally by using lights.

1817: The seat of the Earls of Rosebery, the Gothic Revival **Dalmeny House** contains Scotland's largest collection of Napoleonic memorabilia, including the very pillow on which the vanquished Emperor's head rested during his lying in state.

1824: Already recognising the value of its built heritage, in 1824 Edinburgh became the first city to have its own **municipal fire brigade**. This could explain why around a tenth of all the listed buildings in Scotland are here and why, at least according to the *Daily Telegraph*, at 4,500 it has more of them than any other city in the United Kingdom.

1830: In the days before electric refrigeration, ice needed for preserving food had to be harvested in the winter and stored year-long in insulated, semi-subterranean ice houses. The largest of these to survive is the **Tugnet** at Speyhead in Grampian, part of an old salmon-fishing station owned by the 5th Duke of Richmond and Gordon. Its three barrel-vaulted enclosures are built into naturally sloping ground, cover an area sixty-two feet by fifty-six feet and were last used in the 1950s. (At Murdostone in Strathclyde, for anyone who likes his pigeon fresh, another much smaller one incorporates an ornate little doocot.)

1831: Built to house the dead of a newly rich mercantile class, Glasgow's **Necropolis** contains around 3,500 memorials. It includes a separate section for Jews, but somewhat oddly the architect chose to locate this close to Egyptian vaults and Roman-style catacombs as an uncomfortable reminder of our early ancestors' most zealous persecutors.

1835: **Marischal College**, now part-council offices and part-Aberdeen University, is the second largest granite building in the world, after Madrid's El Escorial.

1849: Built of Mull granite by Robert Louis Stevenson's uncle Alan, the 118-foot-high **Ardnamurchan Lighthouse** adopted the highly fashionable 'style of the Nile' – for a while Egyptian architecture was all the rage – and is still the most westerly building on the British mainland. (Alan Stevenson later designed the Flannen Isles lighthouse, where ahead of its automation three lightkeepers disappeared without trace, thereby inspiring the ghost story *Pharos* by Alice Thompson.)

1857: The oldest surviving music hall in Britain, Glasgow's **Britannia Panopticon** in Trongate was where sixteen-year-old Stan Laurel made his debut in 1906. With room for an audience of 1,500, punters would keep warm by pocketing horse dung from the street outside and then hurling it at duff acts once it had cooled down. A similarly unsanitary habit of peeing on the floorboards is said to have once saved it from burning down.

1868: A small wooden box came to light in Glasgow's Gorbals district and is now kept at the city's **Blessed St John Dun Scotus church**. Labelled *Corpus Valentini Martyris*, it is said to contain the body of St Valentine, the patron saint of florists and greetings card manufacturers.

1875: Now known as **the Wedge**, a house built in Millport on Great Cumbrae off the North Ayrshire coast has been recognised by the editors of the *Guinness Book of World Records* as the world's narrowest house. Approximately twenty feet deep and eleven feet at its widest point, the house has a façade that at forty-seven inches is barely wide enough to accommodate a front door. Despite this it reportedly sleeps four.

1875: The **John O'Groats House Hotel** – one of the most famous in Scotland – is named for a 15th-century Dutchman called Johan or Jan de Groot who ran the ferry across to Orkney. Said to have seven sons, but presumably no wife, he built an octagonal table whose shape is commemorated in the eight-sided tower of the hotel.

1877: Rebuilt after a fire, the 3rd Marquess of Bute's **Mount Stuart** became the first house in the world to have a heated indoor swimming pool. Besides a Victorian passenger lift (still in use) it was also the first in Scotland to include electric lighting, central heating and a telephone system in its original design. At the time of its construction His Grace was conceivably the richest man in Britain, although his adoption of this sort of advanced technology stood somewhat at odds with his well-advertised love of the medieval and mystic.

1890: The **Bellevue Hotel** in Dunbar was constructed along calendar lines with 365 windows, 52 bedrooms and 12 public rooms. Unfortunately this allowed for a mere seven bathrooms to represent the days of the week, although in late-19th-century Scotland this was probably considered highly luxurious.

1900: In Denholm near Jedburgh a three-storey building known as the **Text House** has four tablets on its façade advising passers-by, *Tak tent in time/Ere time be tent/All was others/All will be others.* The work of a local doctor, it was perhaps an attempt to befuddle his next door neighbour, Sir James Murray, editor of the original *New English Dictionary.*

1901: The **Cow Palace** at Borgue in Dumfries and Galloway was long held to be the most well-appointed cattle-shed ever built. Commissioned by a Manchester businessman, and at such great expense that the cows were said to be tethered with solid silver chains, it features an immense central tower modelled on a Scottish baronial castle. But in the way of these things it quickly proved to be wildly impractical.

1902: At Oban, the famous Gateway to the Isles, it's not a fortress that dominates the little town – although ruined Dunstaffnage Castle is nearby – but **McCaig's Tower**. A monstrous but somehow engaging granite rotunda, it was built on Battery Hill by a philanthropic if eccentric banker as a poor copy of the Colosseum at Rome. John Stuart McCaig's intention was to give work to the town's unemployed, but also to commemorate his own family with a museum and gallery within the circle. Nothing came of this, and today the empty shell, which is more than 650 feet in circumference, encloses a garden offering spectacular views.

1907: Albeit in London, another important piece of Scotland's architectural heritage is to be found at **9 Halkin Street**, Belgravia. Once home to the distiller Hugh Morrison (who owned much of Islay), since 1946 it has been home to the Caledonian Club. The members moved here after being bombed out of their clubhouse in St James's Square five years earlier, and unsurprisingly it has the largest collection of single malts of any West End club (and the most members with names beginning Mc or Mac).

1907: An unusual commemoration of a suicide, the **MacDonald**

Monument in Dingwall in Ross-shire is a 100-foot-high square tower built by public subscription to honour the memory of Major General Sir Hector Archibald MacDonald, KCB, DSO. Also known as 'Fighting Mac', Sir Hector was a crofter's son who rose from the ranks after being offered a choice of the Victoria Cross or a commission in the 92nd Gordon Highlanders. Giving him both might have been nice, but choosing the latter he went on to become the hero of Omdurman. Unfortunately, eventually posted to Ceylon, he later fled to Paris and then, after being 'surprised' in a railway carriage with four Sinhalese boys and publicly disgraced, shot himself.

1925: Representing a rare defeat for a powerful man, a few stones are all that remain of the model village of **Leverburgh** on South Harris, the dream of philanthropic 'Soap Man' William Lever. As the 1st Viscount Leverhulme and owner of much of Harris and Lewis, he planned the settlement as part of an expansive £250,000 spending spree designed to improve the lot of the islanders. Islanders were offered a new port, a kipper factory and model dwellings for them and their families, but showed almost no interest. Finally admitting defeat, Lord Leverhulme withdrew after selling the lot to demolition contractors for just £5,000.

1962: An extraordinary **circular house** – hollowed out like a ring doughnut – was commissioned by Earl Granville for a windswept site on the Atlantic coast of North Uist. With concrete walls two feet thick, harled and whitewashed in traditional Hebridean fashion, the house was designed by Sir Martyn Beckett, but in the absence of skilled locals was built by workers brought from Glasgow and rewarded with free shooting and fishing.

1970: When the **Inverkip power station** near Weymss Bay in Inverclyde was completed in 1976 the astonishing 778-foot chimney made it Scotland's tallest free-standing structure, but the whole thing was demolished in a series of controlled explosions in July 2013.

1988: Despite all the hi-tech equipment fitted to Britain's newest nuclear power station, the plant at **Torness** in East Lothian was forced to shut down in May 2013 when the wrong kind of seaweed was spotted floating offshore. As with an earlier shutdown caused by a giant swarm of jellyfish, the seaweed presented a severe choking hazard to the plant's sea water-cooling system.

1997: After a referendum established the need for a new **Scottish Parliament**, a controversial new building was created at a cost to taxpayers of £414 million. Shockingly, the original budget had been closer to £10 million, and by the time of its completion its Catalan architect Enric Miralles had died.

2001: At 416 feet the **Glasgow Tower** is now the tallest tower in Scotland, and the tallest in the world in which the entire building is capable of rotating through 360 degrees. The aerofoil-shaped tower rests upon two-feet-wide bearings, enabling it to rotate under computer control to face into the wind, but unfortunately the technical challenges required to do this are so considerable that the tower has been closed to the public for much if not most of its life.

2004: When the president of the Royal Institute of British Architects suggested Britain's worst eyesores should be demolished, the list included several Scottish nominations. These were the **St James shopping centre** in Edinburgh, Glasgow's **UGC cinema** in Renfrew Street, **St Nicholas House** in Aberdeen and the **Gallowgate** in Glasgow ('a jumble of unrelated rubbish'). Also, most famously, the whole of **Cumbernauld**, where the shopping centre was likened to Kabul.

2005: Creepy **St Peter's College** near Cardross in Argyll and Bute was voted Scotland's most important 20th-century building, despite being a rust-streaked, raw concrete shell. Completed in 1966 but abandoned by 1980, the wreck of the former Roman Catholic seminary is considered by Docomomo (the International

Working Party for Documentation and Conservation of Buildings, Sites and Neighbourhoods of the Modern Movement) to be a building of global significance, and has the highest Category A listing of any building in Scotland.

2012: The *Daily Mail* reported on Lawrence Edmonds' extraordinary quest to become the first person in history (probably) to lick all eight of Scotland's Anglican cathedrals. The twenty-seven-year-old accepted the challenge to visit Aberdeen, Dundee, Edinburgh, Glasgow, Inverness, Millport, Oban and Perth, having previously licked more than forty cathedrals in England. All part of a wager with a friend, it was agreed that the price of failure would be the humiliation of running naked around the precincts of York Minster.

2013: Internet images of **Paisley Abbey** went viral when a photographer visiting the 13th-century former Cluniac monastery noticed a startling resemblance between one of the gargoyles and the eponymous star of the *Alien* movies.

11

Eccentric Scotland

'Eccentricity has always abounded when and where strength of character has abounded; and the amount of eccentricity in a society has generally been proportional to the amount of genius, mental vigour, and moral courage which it contained. That so few now dare to be eccentric, marks the chief danger of the time.'

John Stuart Mill, *On Liberty*

The words 'English' and 'Eccentric' run together so naturally that it is easy to forget that Scotland too has more than its fair share of eccentricity, and from the 17th century to the present day, the country has been comfortably able to hold its own.

Sir Thomas Urquhart (1611–80)

Coming down firmly on the side of the Royalists in the English

Civil War, Thomas Urquhart from Cromarty was knighted for his loyalty to the Crown and is said literally to have died laughing with joy after waiting so long for the happy return of the monarch to the throne.

Like many others Urquhart had fallen on hard times during the Commonwealth. Spending time in the Tower of London at Cromwell's pleasure, and having his estates seized upon his release, he was forced to devote several years to appealing to the authorities for the return of what he felt was rightfully his.

He had a thing about languages too, although his misfortune has been to so baffle linguists that the theories contained in his 'trigonometrical treatise' *Trissotetras* are no better understood today than they were on first publication in 1644. Instead, delighting in the esoteric, the recondite and the arcane – and describing them in a language so dense as to be almost his own – the finished work is considered 'almost impenetrably obscure' even by the erudite compilers of the authoritative *Encyclopaedia Britannica.*

It seemed to matter little that Urquhart included an extensive glossary in the work in which he attempted to explain the meanings of many of the more singular terms he had chosen to employ. Words such as *anfractuosities* and *cathetobasall* featured in the list, the first a reference to 'the cranklings, windings, turnings and involutions belonging to the equisoleary Scheme', while the latter (according to Urquhart) 'is said of the Concordance of Loxogononsphericall Moods, in the Datas of the Perpendicular, and the Base, for finding out of the Maine question'. *Quodomodocunquizingclusterfists*, similarly, was his own word for City bankers.

You get the idea: it's as clear as mud. Perhaps unsurprisingly, his studies eventually led him to devise his own language, one he claimed had precisely sixty-six advantages over English thanks to its use of eleven different genders, ten separate tenses and seven distinct moods. Unfortunately Urquhart refused to publish any more details about it, and so the new, more rational language died when he did. Today only the tiniest fragments of vocabulary remain, most of them the names he gave to animal sounds, including nuzzing (camel), boing (buffalo), coniating (stork), smuttering (monkey), curking (quail), and drintling (turkeys). And beagles don't bark on Planet Urquhart, they 'charm'.

Captain Elliot Elliot Eliott (1712–45)

Eccentrically named, if not in himself particularly odd, the Royal Navy officer owed his bizarre moniker to the fact that his father, Minto-born Sir Gilbert Eliott, 3rd Baronet of Stobs, married the similarly named Eleanor Elliot of Wells and wished to preserve both spellings. The reason for the second 'Elliot' is unknown.

James Burnett, Lord Monboddo (1714–99)

'By far the most learned judge of his time' – and by common repute one of the most respected and eminent of them to sit at the Edinburgh Court of Sessions – Monboddo is nevertheless a chap remembered as much for his odd opinions as for his sound judgements, and when you hear them it's not hard to gauge why. To His Lordship anything modern was a waste of time: if the Ancient Greeks didn't need it and didn't use it then neither did he. Coaches were out of the question, also sedan-chairs, although he would allow his wig to travel in one while he rode to court on horseback. Monboddo indeed went everywhere by horse, but insisted that the ploughs on his Kincardineshire estate be pulled by oxen rather than by horse.

Unfortunately the same logic allowed him to defend slavery – Plutarch had, and that was reason enough for Monboddo – and until his death he failed to grasp why a man of Samuel Johnson's ability would waste it compiling a dictionary of English when Ancient Greek was so much the better tongue.

He wouldn't sit with his fellow judges on the Bench either, preferring for personal reasons to sit down in the body of the court with his clerks. But best of all, he insisted that orang-utans were really men, and that men were really monkeys, a fact concealed by a conspiracy of midwives who cut off the tails of every new-born baby before allowing the mother to see it.

He was serious, too, in 1773 publishing his 'proof' in a volume called *Of the Origin and Progress of Language*, which outlined his theory that orang-utans were also capable of speech and suggested that these humans with tails had first appeared in the Bay of Bengal.

It remained a particular source of frustration to him that, despite observing first-hand the births of all his own children, he had on each occasion been outwitted by the midwife and so failed to see a knife or the evidence of its usage. In old age he thus reluctantly abandoned this part of his theory, although by then the wags knew his name and as a result his reputation as a leading figure in Scottish legal circles continues to suffer.

John Hunter (1728–93)

Born in East Kilbride, the celebrated surgeon was one of the most distinguished scientists of his day, and while not eccentric in himself his collection of medical specimens – sadly now in London – includes a number of decidedly curious exhibits. Among the best are the seven-foot-seven-inch skeleton of Irishman Charles Byrne, the brain of the computer pioneer Charles Babbage and a collection of 17th-century veins and arteries carefully pasted onto wooden boards. These are now in the care of the Royal College of Surgeons.

James Macpherson (1736–96)

Setting forth from Ruthven in Inverness-shire, the writer and poet achieved considerable fame on the publication of a lengthy cycle pithily entitled *Fingal, an Ancient Epic Poem in Six Books, together with Several Other Poems composed by Ossian, the Son of Fingal, translated from the Gaelic Language.*

Macpherson claimed to have discovered and translated the work himself, although the idea that any more than the odd fragment came from the pen of an authentic 3rd-century bard immediately aroused suspicion and then indignation among genuine Gaelic scholars. He was nevertheless able to purchase a considerable country estate on the proceeds of the work, but after his death it was established beyond doubt that he had concocted the whole thing and that the authorities he cited were entirely bogus.

Elspeth Buchan (1738–91)

Establishing her own religious order known as the Buchanites, this potter's wife from Greenock persuaded a priest from Irvine that she was a saint and that he was the son she had been promised in chapter 12 of the biblical book of *Revelations*. The two were rapidly expelled from the congregation, and in 1784 – apparently guided by a Bethlehem-like star – they settled on a farm called New Cample in Dumfriesshire.

Robert Burns the poet dismissed the two adventurers as idle and immoral, but Mrs Buchan continued to claim prophetic inspiration and pretended to confer the Holy Ghost upon her forty-six followers by breathing upon them. She also led them to believe that the millennium would very soon be upon them, but that instead of dying they would be translated to heaven and welcomed by Christ. Her death in 1791 poured cold water on the plans, however, although for a while the clergyman succeeded in persuading her credulous followers that, far from being dead, she was merely in a trance.

Robert Hamilton (1743–1829)

An Aberdeen University professor of natural sciences, Hamilton was famously absent-minded. He would rely on his servants to ensure that he was dressed before leaving the house each morning, and seemed to have no objection to his students' habit of firing peas at him while he was teaching. Formidably intelligent, he gradually developed more of a taste for numbers, and was somehow able to persuade a professor of mathematics at the university to switch places with him. For eighteen years he thus occupied the wrong professorial chair, one for which he was unqualified, but to such good effect that at the end of this period he was appointed to it officially.

RUTHVEN OR RUTHVEN?

In Scotland it's not just the people, and sometimes the correct pronunciation of a name or place can be so bizarre as to make visitors wonder whether it's been done just to catch them out. A few of the most confounding examples are listed below, together with a best-guess as to how they might be said.

Auchinleck	Och-in-Lek
Colquhoun	Ca-HOON
Culzean	Cull-AYN
Dalziel	Dee-ELL (but sometimes DalZEAL)
Hawick	Hoik
Kirkcaldy	Kirk-CAWD-ee
Kirkcudbright	Kirk-COO-bry
MacLachlan	Mac-LOCH-lan
MacLeod	Mac-CLOUD
McKay	Mac-EYE
Menzies	MING-is
Ruthven	RIV-en (in Aberdeenshire)
Ruthven	RUTH-ven (when in Grampian)
Urquhart	ERK-ut

James Robertson (1745?–90)

Nicknamed the Daft Laird, Perthshire-born Robertson was imprisoned for his part in the 1745 Rebellion but released when it was decided that he was harmless. To this he took the greatest exception, and appearing to want nothing more than martyrdom for the cause he went out of his way to be re-arrested. Realising what he was up to, the authorities chose to ignore his deliberate flouting of the law, as for example when he loudly drank to the health of the Pretender in public and spoke treasonably to anyone who would listen.

Eventually he was forced to turn to more conventional crimes in a bid to put himself before a judge, but even this failed when friends stumped up the money for his fine. For Robertson nothing more than a charge of high treason was good enough, but when the judiciary refused to play ball he eventually lost heart and, reinventing himself as a genial, wandering loon, took to the streets of Edinburgh, where he became known for foisting free tobacco and snuff on any passing adults, and small home-made toys on their children.

James Graham (1745–94)

A Scot of obscure origin, and a notorious 18th-century quack, in 1779 James Graham attended medical school but left before qualifying and travelled to London. In a building off the Strand he established his Temple of Health, offering to cure infertility in young, childless couples using a form of music therapy, together with a piece of 'medico-Electrical apparatus' of his own invention.

With the help of an assistant, 'the rosy, athletic and truly gigantic Goddess of Health' – actually the future Lady Hamilton, Nelson's mistress – this proved such a success that he was soon able to move to new, more fashionable premises in Pall Mall. This one he called the Temple of Hymen, and a glass-mounted 'celestial bed' beneath a mirrored ceiling soon had the rich and gullible flocking to seek his cure. Using oriental fragrances and 'aethereal' gases to increase the ardour of the bed's occupants, Graham also attempted to sell his mysterious Elixir of Life for £1,000 a bottle – perhaps a million in today's money – which he claimed would help his clients live to be 150.

Presumably no one took the bait, because by 1784 he was bust and living in Edinburgh. Briefly he attempted to create a sort of cut-price Temple in South Street, but eventually, confined as a lunatic after finding religion, he died in an asylum where he had eaten only vegetables and slept on a horse-hair mattress.

A CLUB FOR GENTLEMEN

Perhaps the nearest Scotland ever got to the celebrated Hellfire Club, the Most Ancient and Most Puissant Order of the Beggar's Benison and Merryland, Anstruther – more commonly just the Beggar's Benison – was founded in the town of that name in 1732.

The name is mysterious but relates to a (fictitious) incident in which James V, disguised as a piper, was rescued by a 'buxom gaberlunzie lass' who tucked up her petticoats and carried him across a flooded river. On the opposite bank, in return for a gold coin, she gave the libidinous monarch her 'benison', a word meaning blessing, although it can be assumed here to be a euphemism for something decidedly more profane. (Merryland, similarly, refers to a genre of Georgian erotic publishing in which the naked female form was likened to a mythical landscape.)

The members were varied but exclusively male and drawn from the professional and upper classes. For more than a hundred years they met at the town's Smugglers Inn to enjoy lectures on the subject of sex, to peruse the club's extensive collection of erotic writings and pictures, to drink from phallic vessels and to gaze upon naked 'posture molls' engaged for this purpose.

Initiation ceremonies formed an important part of club life. Both comical and extremely lewd, such priapic adventures would almost certainly have seen the establishment shuttered and its members gaoled had they been indulged in by any of the lower social classes. Instead offshoots thrived in Edinburgh and Glasgow, with possibly one other in Manchester. Entry was by silver pass (bearing the motto 'Lose No Opportunity'), but by 1836 all were moribund.

Today its papers are held by the University of St Andrews, but sadly not the club president's wig. This was believed to have been woven from the pubic hair of several of Charles II's mistresses but, last seen in 1913 in the offices of a Leith solicitor, it is presumed lost. (The pub still exists too, although it's not the one with the much-photographed sign in the ladies' loo which reads: 'Only cubicle number 4 may be used for (quiet) sexual liaisons. The other cubicles are strictly reserved for lavatory functions.' That one's in Aberdeen.)

John Stewart (1747–1822)

London-born of Scottish parents, 'Walking Stewart' gained his nickname after many years' service to the Honourable East India Company, at the conclusion of which he decided to make his way home to England on foot.

The journey was one he made alone, passing through much of India, Persia, Turkey, Arabia and Abyssinia, and in nearly thirty years of walking he taught himself to speak as many as eight languages fluently. Diversions along the way took him deep into Russia, and as far north as Lapland.

This adventure formed the basis of a book, *Travels over the most interesting parts of the Globe*, which he published in 1790.

He claimed his formidable energy came from inhaling the breath of cows, a practice he maintained on his return to London, where he was easily spotted thanks to a habit of dressing in Armenian national costume.

To publicise the book and his other writings Stewart conceived a scheme to have his name carved in giant letters on Ireland's Atlantic cliffs, the idea being that anyone passing by ship would have their curiosity aroused and seek to know more. Needless to say this never happened but, convinced that his writings were of lasting and important value, he prevailed upon a friend to translate them into Latin in case the reading and writing of English went out of fashion.

In 1822, Stewart took laudanum and died quietly in a rented room off London's Trafalgar Square, since when all his books have gone out of print.

Jamie 'Baillie' Duff (? – 1788)

Duff first came to the public's attention after entering a horse race at Leith. He didn't own a horse and couldn't borrow one, but ran the course barefoot while whipping himself with a crop and making suitably horse-like noises. The public enjoyed the spectacle a good deal, later giving him the nickname Baillie for his habit of dressing like the civic officers responsible for keeping order in Scottish burghs.

For more than forty years Duff also made a habit of gatecrashing private funerals, often leading the procession to the church but being careful to behave and dress respectably with a black cravat and matching hat and weeper (the name given to a badge of mourning popular at this time).

In Edinburgh it was said that 'no solemnity of that kind could take place in the city without being graced by his presence', and he often picked up a shilling from the family for his trouble. Indeed, 'by keeping a sharp look-out for prospective funerals,' one contemporary noted, 'Jamie succeeded in securing almost all the enjoyment which the mortality of the city was capable of affording'. As enjoyment here almost certainly refers to his share of the whisky traditionally dispensed after Scottish funerals, Duff may not have been quite as daft as he is sometimes painted.

Charles Piazzi Smyth (1819–1900)

Scotland's Astronomer Royal for more than forty years, Smyth was based at Calton Hill Observatory in Edinburgh and has a crater on the moon named after him. He pioneered the technique of infra-red astronomy and, realising that cities were poor places to make astronomical observations, in 1856 he established the world's first high-altitude observatory at what is now Las Palmas Observatory in the Canaries.

Unfortunately in later life he became obsessed by the pyramids of Egypt and pyramidology, and this has tended to overshadow his more orthodox scientific work. Today he is recalled as the only Fellow of the Royal Society ever to resign after having a paper rejected for publication, his reputation largely trashed by his determination to pursue his own brand of mystical pseudo-science.

In particular, Smyth claimed that measurements he obtained from the Great Pyramid of Giza had led him to the discovery of an ancient unit of length, the pyramid inch (equivalent to 1.001 normal inches), as well as a pyramid pint, a sacred cubit, and the pyramid scale of temperature. These he maintained were divine measures, handed down by Noah's son Shem, and thus incontrovertible proof that God had directed the construction of the pyramids.

According to Smyth, the Great Pyramid was a repository of prophecies that could be revealed only by detailed measurements of the structure. His findings also seemed to imply that the rival metric system was the work of the devil, or at least of French atheists. This modest appeal to popular patriotism was unable to prevent Smyth and his work being widely discredited once his promises that the Second Coming was due in 1882, 1892 and then in 1911 all failed to materialise.

Fortunately, by this time Smyth was dead, having chosen, unsurprisingly, to be buried beneath a small stone pyramid topped by a Christian cross.

William Gallacher MP (1881–1965)

Always known as 'Willie,' in 1935 Paisley-born Gallacher was elected as Westminster's only communist, an affiliation that now looks decidedly eccentric in the light of more recent events. His apprenticeship for the job was similarly unorthodox and included a period in prison during the Great War (for publishing material contrary to the Defence of the Realm Act), and another twelve-month sentence in 1925 following his prosecution under the Incitement to Mutiny Act (1797).

A co-founder of the Communist Party of Great Britain, Willie had contested three different Scottish constituencies in five successive elections before finally being returned as the member for West Fife – on his third attempt – in 1935. He held the seat until 1950, but Cold War tensions did for him and his party in the end. Strongly identified with the enemy, no more communists have been elected since.

Interestingly, Gallacher's unseating (by a landslide majority) was at the hands of another Willie, Willie Hamilton, almost certainly the most anti-monarchist MP of the 20th century. Remembered now only for his campaigns against the Windsor dynasty, he famously characterised the queen as a 'clockwork doll', branded her sister a floozy and called Prince Charles a twerp. Despite all this he retained the seat for nearly forty years but, following his rejection by the voters, polled just 8% of the vote after moving to England to have another shot at a parliamentary career. Curiously, in old age he developed a soft spot for the queen mother, whom he thought 'a superb royal trouper'.

Ivor Cutler (1923–2006)

The talented son of Jewish immigrants who fled to Glasgow to escape the Tsarist pogroms, the eccentric poet, singer and story-teller was born within 100 yards of Ibrox Park and, with an ear for an anecdote, always maintained that his first scream was synchronous with a Rangers goal.

After working briefly as a Rolls-Royce fitter, even more briefly as an RAF navigator during the war, and then as a teacher, he travelled to London where, working as a songwriter, he was spotted by Paul McCartney and invited to play a small role as a bus conductor called Buster Bloodvessel in the Beatles film *Magical Mystery Tour.*

Soon he was being fêted by many well-known names, including the philosopher Bertrand Russell, DJ John Peel and his fellow Glaswegian Billy Connolly, and visitors to his flat at the foot of Parliament Hill in north London found it to be every bit as eccentric as its occupier. Besides ivory cutlery – an engaging if obvious pun on his name – the clutter included his trademark harmonium, a large wax ear nailed to the wall and hats adorned with dozens of badges. The latter would be used to conceal his baldness, although he frequently observed that *sur le volcan ne pousse pas l'herbe* (grass does not grow on a volcano).

As an enthusiastic member of the Noise Abatement Society, Cutler famously forbade his fans from whistling any of his tunes; he also taught himself to speak Chinese because (he said) the text-books were cheaper than those in Japanese. His preferred mode of transport was also singular: an old fashioned sit-up-and-beg bicycle that he would pedal around London, dressed in plus fours. While out and about it was his habit to carry a piece of chalk with him and to use this to draw cartoon faces on the pavement whenever he found any dog poo.

12

Ceremonial Scotland

'Government isn't organized for efficiency, nor to serve the people. It is organized to provide jobs for the boys.'

Syracuse Herald, October 1913

Sadly, we have seen the last of many splendid-sounding official appointments: the Keeper of the Royal Firebuckets has gone; so too the Embellisher of Letters to the Eastern Princes. But Scotland's long history means there are still plenty of jobs for the boys – and it's nearly always boys – and still plenty to celebrate for lovers of the ancient, obscure and arcane.

The Bailie of the Abbey Court of Holyrood

Bailies were originally responsible for administering justice on behalf of the great territorial magnates, and today this unique survivor oversees the efficient management of the Palace of

Holyrood and of a team of High Constables charged with keeping order when the sovereign is in residence.

Each new Bailie is still appointed by the Duke of Hamilton, the dukes having been appointed Hereditary Keepers of the Palace in 1646. Back then just one constable was required to maintain order in a building that was at once a royal palace, a parliament, a prison and a place of sanctuary. Today, despite our living in apparently more peaceful times, the modern establishment employs no fewer than thirty, each furnished with a blue velvet suit, a hat and a narrow sword in a black leather scabbard.

Captain General of the Queen's Bodyguard for Scotland

Known as Gold Stick for short, the holder of this important office commands the prestigious Royal Company of Archers. This received its charter in 1704 from Queen Anne, but as long ago as 1676 it had been noted that, having been neglected for many years, the 'noble and useful recreation of archers' was revived by 'several Noblemen and Gentlemen' who assembled themselves into a company.

It might be recalled that an earlier monarch, James VI, thought so highly of the toxopholite arts that he went so far as to ban football in order to encourage his subjects to take up their bows and arrows instead. Today that same enthusiasm is much in evidence, albeit on a modest scale, and each year during the monarch's sojourn in their capital members of the Company parade in smart uniforms of Border Green.

Regular contests between the archers are still held using special targets known as clouts. These are no longer situated beneath the prominent rocky outcrop on the city's skyline we know as Arthur's Seat, which is a shame as its original name is thought to have been 'Archers', as this is where the men used to relax between rounds.

Captain of Dunstaffnage

Officially the Hereditary Keeper of Dunstaffnage Castle, which has long been ruined, the holder of the post is still required by order of the courts to spend at least three nights of the year in this once mighty and impregnable fortress overlooking the Firth of Lorn.

Strategically located on Scotland's western approaches, the castle has played an important part in the political and military history of the area and is thought to date back to the mid-13th century. (Some place its origins even further back, to the time of a mythical King Ewin some 2,000 years ago, but the evidence for this is lacking.)

Some indication of its importance can be drawn from the fact that the Stone of Destiny – or of Scone – is thought to have come from here originally, its more common name referring to its removal much later to Scone. (And where, following its recovery from Westminster, it once more resides.) The castle was also captured by Robert the Bruce, and for a while the garrison there held Flora MacDonald prisoner (see Ghostly Scotland). Today the Keeper for his three nights stays as a guest of Historic Scotland, custodians of the castle, which is now Crown property.

Cock o' the North

An extraordinary title with a dismal history, it was coined for the 4th Earl of Huntly, who died on the field in 1562 in defeat at the Battle of Corrichie, either of apoplexy or strangulation (the truth is not known).

As Lieutenant General of the North and Warden of the Marches, he had earlier been appointed regent by James V when the latter left for France to find a wife, and for a while he did a fine job of keeping the dastardly English at bay. Because of this, and as an effective commander, he was nicknamed 'Cock o' the North' by Mary, Queen of Scots, although he was subsequently outmanoeuvred by jealous rivals and fell from grace.

His death on the battlefield was nevertheless considered heroic, and as a tribute his descendants – long since elevated to the rank of marquess – continue to be known by this singularly colourful title.

The First Foot

This is the first person a Scottish bride sees on her way to the wedding, and he or she is traditionally rewarded with a coin and some whisky before being required to join the bridal procession.

Hereditary Banner Bearer for Scotland & Hereditary Bearer of the National Flag of Scotland

From the early 12th century the right to bear the Royal Banner of Scotland during State and martial occasions has been jealously guarded. In 1910, after literally centuries of wrangling between two families claiming the same legal right, the Court of Claims finally found in favour of the Scrymgeours and against the rival Maitland family, who were ordered to meet the expenses of the long legal battle.

The case might have ended there were it not for the intervention of the Lord Lyon King of Arms (see below), who encouraged both parties to meet in a spirit of compromise. It took until 1953, but eventually an agreement was reached whereby the Scrymgeours (as Earls of Dundee) retained the right to carry the Royal Banner, while the descendants of the rival Maitlands (now Dukes of Lauderdale) were granted responsibility for Scotland's national flag, the Saltire.

Hereditary Falconer

An enjoyable pastime but once truly the sport of kings, falconry has fallen in and out of fashion but continues to carry with it some extraordinary perks for a few of those involved. South of the border the Hereditary Grand Falconer – a sinecure belonging to the Dukes of St Albans, as descendants of Nell Gwyn – enjoys the right to drive a carriage along Rotten Row in Hyde Park, a privilege otherwise restricted to the sovereign.

In Scotland there is no equivalent, although since Stuart times the post of Royal Falconer has been equally sought after, carrying with it as it does the chance of close proximity to the Crown and possible influence. Today the position of Hereditary Falconer is held by the 24th Lord Borthwick, a descendent of the 1st Lord who was raised to the peerage in the 15th century and – it is to be supposed – was granted the honour in return for services rendered.

Unsurprisingly, given the span of time involved, there are no documents confirming any of this, but it seems likely as it is known that various Borthwicks have gone far beyond the normal call in serving their sovereigns. The 1st Lord Borthwick, for example, was deprived of his liberty for nearly three years after offering himself as a hostage in place of James I, and at Flodden his grandson, the 3rd Lord, fought and died alongside James IV. For this the right to fly a bird or two seems a modest enough reward.

FIVE ODD HOGMANAY TRADITIONS

There's no New Year like a Scots New Year, and for many it's the time when some of Scotland's oddest traditions spring to the fore. Not all of them are that old – or perhaps that should be auld – but neither will they be forgot once you've seen them.

Burning of the Clavie

In parts of the old county of Elginshire they get two bites of the cherry. The townspeople of Burghead have celebrated New Year twice – on 1 January and then again ten days later – since the 18th century, when the Gregorian calendar replaced the Julian, robbing citizens of a few vital days. To celebrate, they light a barrel of tar – the clavie – which is then carried round the town and up Dorrie Hill before being allowed to burn out and tumble down the hill. Gathering around the smoking remains is supposed to bring good luck for the year ahead.

Redding

What down south they call a spring clean, redding traditionally takes place ahead of Hogmanay itself and should be completed before the midnight bells. As well as a clearing of all firegrates, and a settling of debts, redding involves a ritual burning of sweet-smelling juniper to ward off disease and disaster in the coming year.

Swinging Fireballs

Stonehaven celebrates the New Year with fire too, and on 31 December the town assembles to form a procession, while those brave enough to do so swing burning balls of chicken wire and cloth around their heads before flinging them into the sea. Designed to ward off witches, and looking decidedly ancient, the practice is nevertheless supported by little if any documentation to suggest its origin is earlier than 1908.

The Kirkwall Ba'

Football like it used to be, which is to say brutal, chaotic and seemingly undisciplined, Orkney's contribution to the supposedly beautiful game is played on New Year's Day with a leather ball stuffed with cork and the whole of the islands' capital thrown open to play.

The Loony Dook

This decidedly new tradition sees South Queensferry folk gathering on 1 January to take a bracing dip in the waters of the Forth. In 1987 the first such event attracted just a handful of locals, but today people come from far and wide – sometimes even from warm countries – to test their mettle in this singular fashion.

Keeper of the Signet

Whilst many ancient posts disappeared with the legal changes ordered by James V in the 1530s, and then again following the 1707 Act of Union and the events at Culloden, one of the more colourful survivors is the Lord Clerk Register's responsibility for the sovereign's signet ring.

Dating from a time when the official imprint in a wax seal would have provided all the proof an illiterate populace needed of a king's authority, it was a vitally important role. Overseeing the so-called Writers to the Signet – the clerks responsible for drafting documents due to go before the court – and authorising their work with the imprint of the ring, the Keeper continues to this day to validate all business conducted by the Scottish courts.

Knight Marischal

The colourful office of Knight Marischal was created in 1633 for the Scottish coronation of Charles I at Scone, and it was a paid post until the Public Offices (Scotland) Act of 1817 determined that no more payments would be made. The 11th Duke of Hamilton nevertheless retained it until 1863. Since his death the post has not been filled, although as no move was made to abolish it the role is presumed still to exist.

(A similar post, that of Marischal, served as custodian of the Royal Regalia of Scotland, and the holder charged to protect the king's person at Parliament, but this disappeared in 1715.)

Lord High Commissioner to the General Assembly of the Church of Scotland

The heyday of the Lord High Commissioners arrived in the early 1600s when King James VI travelled south of the border, becoming James I and the King of England. From 1603 until 1707, when the two countries became one, the Commissioners represented the absent sovereign in parliament and the established church. Today, needless to say, the position is purely ceremonial, although vestigial perks include the right to be known as 'Your Grace' and to fly the standard of the Scottish sovereign. Two flunkeys are also always in attendance on the Commissioner, a Pursebearer and Macebearer, not dissimilar in style and function to those who accompany the Lord Mayor of the City of London.

Lord High Constable

Commanding the Doorward Guard of Partisans, the oldest body guard in Britain, the role of Lord High Constable is another hereditary post and has been held by the Hays of Errol since the Battle of Bannockburn in 1314.

On that occasion Sir Gilbert de la Haye offered his support to the Bruce, since when his descendants as chiefs of the Clan Hay have been promoted to the rank of earl or on two occasions the rank of a countess in her own right. They have managed to retain the post despite a number of reverses, including periods when their adherence to the Old Faith and support for Bonnie Prince Charlie threatened to unseat them once and for all.

For centuries the holder of the post was the supreme officer of the Scottish Army, second only to the king. He or she also sat as the chief judge of the High Court of Constabulary, and from the late 13th century was empowered to preside in all cases of rioting, disorder, bloodshed and murder committed within four miles of the king's person, his council or his parliament.

Today all such powers have been removed, but with the afore-mentioned Doorward Guard working in concert with the High Constable of Holyrood (see above), the Lord High Constable as their commander takes precedence over all other titles bar those of the royal family. This small courtesy serves as a quiet reminder of his once mighty status.

Lord Lyon King of Arms

Whilst sharing many similarities, the heraldry of Scotland differs markedly from that of England and Wales and falls under the control of the Lord Lyon King of Arms. The sole grantor of armorial bearings to clan chiefs and other prominent personages, he sits as a judge in the country's only court of chivalry and presides over important matters of state ceremonial.

The post is ancient, dating back at least to 1377, when documents show a *Leo Regi Heraldorum* or Lion Herald receiving payment from the Exchequer for services rendered. It has also been suggested that a Lord Lyon played a significant role at the coronation of Robert II in 1371, although the feline reference may be considerably older, a nod to William the Lion who reigned from 1165 to 1214 and established early anti-English links with the French.

Representative Peers

For more than 250 years Scottish noblemen and women had no right to sit in the House of Lords, and instead had to elect sixteen of their number to act as their representatives. (The English were understandably worried the Scots would flood the place, as there are so many more Scottish peers than English ones relative to their respective populations.) This changed with the 1963 Peerage Act, which allowed all of them to take their places in the upper house, but they then lost this right (along with all the other hereditaries) after the Blair government's reforms of 1999 handed the chamber over to the day boys and other largely political placemen.

Royal Handwasher of Cramond Bridge

An otherwise unremarkable crossing-place between Edinburgh and the Forth Road Bridge, it was on Cramond Bridge that James V (some say James II) was rescued from a gang of muggers by a farmer working in a nearby field.

Jock Howieson or Houison heard the affray and ran to the defence of the traveller (whom he did not recognise), apparently with no regard for his own safety. Having chased off the footpads and taken the traveller back to his own cottage to clean up, he then accompanied him back to the city. Explaining on the way that he was employed on one of the king's farms at Braehead, Houison was asked what would make him happier than anything on earth. He confessed that he could think of nothing better than owning the land he worked, and the two men laughed over such a wild idea.

When they parted the farmer still had no idea to whom he was speaking, and believed the traveller to be no more than the most minor court official. As a thank-you for his timely intervention, Houison was offered a private tour of the State Rooms at Palace of Holyrood, and took up the offer a few days later.

He was met by his new friend, who asked whether he would like to see the king. He said yes, of course, and was ushered into the Great Hall where he was assured that the king would be instantly recognisable as the only person present wearing a hat.

Houison looked around – the place was rammed full of courtiers – but could see no one wearing a hat except his friend. Feeling the joke had gone on long enough the king finally admitted his identity, and made Houison a present of the farm on which he had been labouring. It was given, he said, on the condition that Houison would present the monarch with a basin, ewer and towel with which he could wash his hands whenever he passed by this bridge.

It's a charming story and, centuries on, the tradition still continues. Following her accession to the throne in 1952 Queen Elizabeth II met with Jock's descendent, Peter Houison Craufurd, 28th Laird of Craufurdland Castle, and on his death in 2012 the mantle passed to his son Alex as the 29th.

Up Helly Aa and the Beards of Bressay

Unfortunately, and no matter how ancient the ceremony, it seems that health and safety can still rudely intervene. On the Shetland island of Bressay they've been celebrating their Viking heritage for hundreds of years by burning a replica longboat in the annual fire festival known as Up Helly Aa. Participants in the festivities like to grow long straggly beards in order to look more authentic, but in January 2014 it was reported that because of this the local volunteer fire brigade was having to be stood down. Facial hair apparently makes it impossible for the firefighters to use breathing apparatus, forcing the temporary closure of the fire station until the modern-day Vikings had done their thing.

13

Fighting Scotland

'Warte bis der Schotte kommt'
An old German saying designed to scare children:
Wait until the Scot comes and gets ye!

The Real Braveheart:
Never Let the Facts Spoil a Good Story

In box office terms the most successful Scottish war film of all time, Mel Gibson's violently Anglophobic epic won five Oscars, but is nevertheless so riddled with factual errors that in 2009 the *Times* newspaper placed it second in its list of the historically most inaccurate films of all time. The many howlers cineastes are expected to overlook include:

- 'Braveheart' was actually the nickname of Robert the Bruce and not William Wallace.
- Most of the extras in the battle scenes are Irishmen not Scottish, as much of the filming took place near Dublin, and the film's only genuine Irish character is played Scots-born David O'Hara.

148

- The film suggests that, while canoodling with Princess Isabella, sneaky Wallace somehow fathered Edward III. In fact, Edward wasn't born until November 1312, seven years after Wallace's execution.

- It is also highly unlikely that the French Isabella would have warned Wallace about the upcoming Battle of Falkirk, as she does in the film. She was only three years old at the time, had never visited the British Isles and almost certainly didn't speak English.

- The famous quotation, 'Every man dies, not every man really lives', comes not from this Wallace at all but from an unrelated 19th-century poet called William Wallace.

- Woad, the blue body paint that features so heavily during the battle scenes, went out of fashion in Roman times, which is to say at least 800 years before Wallace was born.

- Despite the evidence of the film English soldiers wore no uniforms at this time, and the clan tartans sported by the opposing side were also not due to make an appearance in Scotland for literally hundreds more years.

- The crucially important Battle of Stirling Bridge is completely misrepresented, showing long lines of soldiers on an open battlefield, when in reality the English and Scots faced each other across the Forth River. Heavily outnumbered, the small numbers of English soldiers who began to cross the narrow wooden bridge were slaughtered by the Scots or drowned while trying to escape.

- Wallace's real-life wife was called Marian, not Murron.

- In the film Wallace is captured at Edinburgh Castle, but in truth he was taken prisoner at Robroyston, now a suburb of Glasgow, before being turned over to the English and executed at Smithfield in London. After being hanged and drawn, his four quarters were displayed in Newcastle upon Tyne, Berwick-upon-Tweed, Stirling, and Perth. The head remained down south, stuck on a pike on London Bridge.

WHY COLDSTREAM:
A SCOTS NAME FOR AN ENGLISH REGIMENT?

As the oldest regiment in the regular Army in continuous active service, the Coldstream Guards can trace their roots back to 1650. As part of Oliver Cromwell's New Model Army, fighting for Parliament in the English Civil War, the troops were at this time known as Monck's Regiment of Foot.

A decade later General Monck crossed the River Tweed at Coldstream in support of Charles II, and the regiment changed its name. Entering royal service just after the Grenadier Guards (although the older of the two units), they are therefore strictly speaking second in seniority, but retain the motto *Nulli Secundus*, meaning 'Second to None'.

The Secrets of Scapa Flow

- A vast natural harbour, it takes its name from the Old Norse *Skalpaflói*, meaning 'bay of the long isthmus', and describes an area of 120 square miles where more than a thousand years ago Viking longships sought shelter.

- In July 1914 Winston Churchill, as First Lord of the Admiralty, ordered the British Grand Fleet to leave Portland for the relative safety of Scapa Flow in the Orkneys. With characteristic style he later described an eighteen-mile procession 'of gigantic castles of steel, wending their way through the misty, shining sea like giants bowed in anxious thought'.

- The base was reinforced with an array of minefields, coastal artillery, blockships and concrete barriers, and of the two attempts by German U-boats to penetrate the defences and enter the harbour neither was successful. The first sub was rammed by a trawler and sunk, the second destroyed by remote-controlled mines.

- Following the German defeat in 1918 more than seventy German warships were held captive at Scapa Flow. After a nine-month stand-off Rear Admiral Ludwig von Reuter, mistakenly believing that hostilities were about to be renewed, unilaterally took the decision to scuttle the vessels rather than risk them falling into the host country's hands. Nine of his sailors died as the British tried desperately – but in vain – to prevent the enemy ships going down. Shot in the chaos and confusion, they are generally held to be the last casualties of the Great War.

- In all fifty-two ships of the German High Fleet were deliberately sunk by their crew in this way – 400,000 tons of steel – including eleven great battleships, making it the worst loss in history of shipping in a single day. Over the next twenty years forty-five of them were successfully salvaged from the cold waters before the Second World War intervened in September 1939.

- Once again Scapa Flow, distant as it is from newly hostile German airfields, was to provide an important redoubt for the Royal Navy. However, the old defences were no longer in good repair, and in October 1939 U-boat *U-47* was able to enter and torpedo HMS *Royal Oak* with a loss of 833 British lives. An attack by German bombers three days later prompted the construction of new 'Churchill Barriers' (see the Tourist Scotland chapter for more on this).

- Today the few remaining German wrecks and other features at Scapa Flow make Orkney one of the best dive sites in the UK, although licences are required by all divers and war graves such as the remains of the *Royal Oak* are protected.

THE BLUESHIRTS OF SHAME

The classic image of British fascism between the wars is of Sir Oswald Mosley brawling with his blackshirts in London's Jewish East End. But many Scots embraced extreme right-wing politics in the 1920s and 1930s too, with the blue shirts of the pioneering British Fascisti organisation a familiar sight on Scotland's streets.

- Huge numbers of women were attracted to far-right politics, and indeed the founding members of British Fascisti in 1923 included Miss Rotha Lintorn-Orman, fresh from the Scottish Women's Hospital Corps, and Lady Menzies of Menzies.

- Around the same time, the nationalist poet Hugh MacDiarmid was promoting his own brand of tartan fascism and trying to launch what he called Clann Albain. This was an openly 'neo-fascistic' paramilitary body, which he envisaged leading the fight for Scotland's freedom, and like other nationalists he saw in Hitler an opportunity to get even with the English.

- The 8th Earl of Glasgow was another enthusiastic supporter of the movement, apparently concerned that democracy was damaging his privileges and lifestyle, while the 21st Earl of Erroll was often to be seen wearing fascist insignia on his sporran.

- In 1933 St Andrews University Union Debating Society invited German Otto Wagner to propose the motion, 'This House approves of the Nazi Party, and congratulates it on its splendid work in the reformation of Germany' – which the members subsequently passed with a very clear majority.

- The same year an officer in the Seaforth Highlanders, Norman Baillie-Stewart, was detained in the Tower of

London and court-martialled after selling secrets to a German contact for £90. Sentenced to five years' penal servitude, 'the Officer in the Tower' went to Germany on his release, and after selling his story to the *Daily Express* was prosecuted again for pro-Nazi activities and got another five years.

- In 1934 more than 3,000 people in Dumfriesshire joined the first Scottish gathering of Mosley's British Union of Fascists, the county even going so far as to establish a fascists-only football league. Among those who fell under the fascist spell were the 12th Earl of Mar, the 7th Duke of Montrose and the 8th Duke of Buccleuch, the latter at least recognising that he should perhaps resign his post as Lord Steward of the Royal Households.

- Around the same time a special grey fascist tartan was devised to be worn as a kilt. (Conventional tartans were ruled out on the grounds that fascist policy was to be inclusive, meaning it had to embrace 'all clans and classes'.) Before long five of the fifteen branches of the UK Fascist Party were to be found in Scotland – in Edinburgh, Aberdeen, Dundee, Glasgow and Greenock.

- In 1936 an organisation known as the Kaledonian Klan repeatedly fought running battles through the streets of the poorer areas in Edinburgh. In Cowgate, Grassmarket and Canongate the targets were mostly Catholics rather than Jews, but the scenes were otherwise strongly reminiscent of Mosley and his thugs running riot in in east London.

- Two years later a hairdresser from Dundee, Jessie Wallace Jordan, was convicted of spying for the Nazis. Caught sketching Scotland's coastal defences, she was shopped to the authorities by her cleaner. After finding a detailed map of the River Tay in the Kinloch

Street salon, mother-of-four Mary Curran was given £1 as a reward and told to keep *schtum*.

- In 1940 the dishonourable member for Peebles, Archibald Maule Ramsay, became the only MP to be interned during the war. A descendent of the Earls of Dalhouse, this rabid anti-Semite and keen conspiracy theorist had been offered the post of Nazi Gauleiter for Scotland in the event of a successful German invasion. To the end he believed that Jews had deliberately sought to make a war with Germany inevitable.

- Donald 'Derrick' Grant from Alness spent the war broadcasting Nazi propaganda under the banner of Radio Caledonia, which was based in a Berlin suburb. Released from prison in late 1947, Scotland's own Lord Haw-Haw returned to Easter Ross where he was stoned by his former neighbours and run out of the village. He died in London in the 1980s.

- In 2001 it was revealed that nearly sixty years earlier wartime code breakers had intercepted a signal sent to Berlin suggesting a Scottish-Nazi alliance 'as a weapon in the fight against the gross materialism of the capitalistic-communistic union of English, Americans, Bolsheviks etc.'. The authors of the memo, who have never been identified, requested that Germany not bomb Scottish targets, and said they hoped to establish a 'Scottish republic' while England was paralysed by panic.

Britain's Bravest Family

A resident of Dingwall, Shane Gough, 5th Viscount Gough, enjoys the unique distinction of having three recipients of the Victoria Cross in his family tree. His heroic kinsmen include two brothers: General Sir Charles Gough VC, who was present at the Siege of Lucknow during the Indian Mutiny in 1857; and General Sir Hugh Gough VC, who the same year 'charged across a swamp, and captured two guns, although defended by a vastly superior body of the enemy'. Finally, the former's son, Brigadier General Sir John Edmond Gough VC, during the Third Somaliland Expedition in 1903, put himself into the greatest danger whilst attempting to get a wounded officer onto a camel and out of range of the enemy's guns.

Scotland Takes to the Air

- Scotland's leading air ace of the Second World War was Archie McKellar from Paisley, one of the RAF's famous Few. With twenty-one confirmed kills, he died when his Hawker Hurricane was shot down near Adisham in Kent.

- McKellar's death was logged on 1 November 1940, the day after the official end of the Battle of Britain. This decisive conflict was famously fought over the fields of southern England but directed by a Scot. Head of Fighter Command, Air Chief Marshal Sir Hugh 'Stuffy' Dowding was born in Moffat to the wife of a former master at Fettes College.

- Married to George Douglas-Hamilton, 10th Earl of Selkirk, in 1947, Audrey Sale-Barker – 'Wendy' to her friends – is one of the war's unsung heroines, and flew scores of fighters as a member of the Air Transport Auxiliary. Responsible for delivering combat aircraft to front-line aerodromes, in her spare time she was British Alpine ski champion, and once flew a biplane from London down the length of Africa to Cape Town.

- The Fleet Air Arm's most decorated pilot, Leith-born Captain Eric 'Winkle' Brown – ninety-five and still going strong – has flown more aircraft types than anyone else in history. With a total of 487 (including fifty-three captured from the Germans) he also holds the world record for the most aircraft-carrier landings at 2,407.

- Today Scotland's most spectacular air force memorial is a full-size replica of a Supermarine Spitfire. Installed on the northern perimeter of the airfield at RAF Grangemouth in Stirlingshire, it honours local pilots as well as Poles, Canadians, Australians, New Zealanders and Americans who were killed while serving with a Scottish unit there.
- In a melancholy echo of a celebrated wartime mission, in February 2014 members of the 617 'Dambuster' Squadron – made famous by the celebrated bouncing-bomb raid on Germany – returned to RAF Lossiemouth from Afghanistan for the last time. The unit is due to be disbanded for the third time in its heroic, action-packed history

---

THE RIGHT STUFF

One of only very few RAF pilots to hold the Victoria Cross, William Reid (1921–2001) was a blacksmith's son from Baillieston, Lanarkshire. In 1943, having lost his navigator in an attack by German fighters, Reid went on to complete a raid on Düsseldorf before somehow nursing his badly damaged Lancaster LM360 home to save the lives of his crew. In 1952 he married but was too modest to tell his wife about the medal, and at auction in 2009 this was sold for £384,000, a record for any awarded to a British subject.

Simply Scottish: A Better Way of Killing

Claymore

From the Gaelic *Claidheamh Mòr*, meaning 'great sword', the name describes a two-handed weapon with an overall length of around five feet. In use from the 13th century, and reportedly still striking fear into Scotland's enemies 500 years later, the longest on record is an astonishing nine feet top to tip, weighing in at more than 23 lb. Assuming one can lift it and swing it, the idea is to prevent an opponent from getting anywhere within striking distance.

Dirk

By contrast, Scotland's other famous blade is rarely more than a foot in length, making it a highly effective thrusting weapon. Dating from the 16th century, and ideal for close hand-to-hand combat, it is not to be confused with the *sgian-dubh*, which is worn as a traditional part of Highland dress and commonly used for eating fruit, fish, meat and cheese.

Donald Dinnies

Great War slang for heavy artillery shells, the name is an affectionate reference to the strongman who dominated Scotland's Highland Games for as much as two decades. The real Dinnie (1837–1916) was from Birse near Aboyne, and with a competitive career spanning five decades he is reckoned to have taken part in more than 11,000 challenges. Besides the usual Highland fun these included carrying two boulders with a combined weight of 775 pounds across the River Dee. (Both stones can still be seen outside the Potarch Hotel on the south bank of the river not far from Kincardine O'Neil.)

Gunpowder

The Scots didn't invent the stuff, but in 1460, at Roxburgh Castle, James II achieved a strange kind of immortality by going on record as the first sovereign anywhere in the world ever to be killed in an explosion. The unfortunate monarch had been standing too close to one of the castle's cannon (known as the lion) when it blew up, removing his leg with fatal consequences.

Kent

Exceptionally crude but clearly quite effective, a kent was a mighty oak cudgel, weighted with lead and as much as five feet in length. Rarely if ever seen on the battlefield, most were home-made and in the 1700s many were bloodied during altercations between whisky smugglers on the Ayrshire coast and the revenue men sent to stop them.

Mine Detector

The world's first practical and reliable mine detector was invented in Scotland, the creation of Lt Jozef Stanislaw Kosacki and produced in response to a British War Office competition in the early years of the Second World War. Kosacki was a signals officer with the 1st Polish Army Corps, stationed at Tenstsmuir near Tayport in Fife, and his winning design, rushed into production, is thought to have doubled the speed of British penetration through heavily mined areas. Fifty years later the same basic machine was still being used by British troops in the First Gulf War.

Mons Meg

Standing proud upon the granite core of an extinct volcano, Edinburgh Castle's most famous exhibit is probably mighty Mons Meg, a medieval bombard and as such a fearsome siege weapon. Made for the bellicose Duke of Burgundy in 1449, it remained in use for more than 200 years, but was then retired after exploding in the presence of the future James II of England. The reasons for the incident are unclear, but at the time the English were accused of deliberately overloading the weapon because they had nothing quite as magnificent themselves. (Incidentally, the last shot ever fired in anger from the castle was in 1745, when an unknown red-coat took a few pot-shots at supporters of Bonnie Prince Charlie passing down below.)

Sheltron

Also known as a schiltrom, meaning a compact body of troops or a pike formation. It was commonly seen during the Wars of Scottish Independence in the late 13th and early 14th centuries, although the term may be many hundreds of years older. Seen to good effect in *Braveheart* (see above), the tactic looked formidable but in reality was highly vulnerable to skilled archers such as the Welsh longbowman and English archers the Scots encountered in the Battle of Falkirk.

X-Craft

A few feet off the beach at Aberlady Bay in East Lothian are the twisted remains of two midget submarines. Known as X-Craft and visible at low tide, they were towed here at the end of the Second World War and used as targets by the Royal Air Force. In service each would have weighed approximately thirty tons, the crew of three or four propelled by a similar engine to that used in London's iconic double-decker buses.

Several saw action during the D-Day landings, but their most famous mission was the one sent to destroy the German battleship *Tirpitz*. Of the six despatched to her berth in Norway two successfully laid their explosive charges, and the crippled vessel was then sunk by 12,000 lb bombs dropped by Avro Lancasters of the RAF. One of the vessels also made it into the *Guinness Book of World Records* when a Helensburgh man, Lt Commander Bill Morrison, made what was later recognised as the deepest unaided escape from a stricken submarine after his modified XE11 sank to a depth of more than 200 feet in Loch Striven.

Today, with the two craft at Aberlady Bay considered to be beyond restoration, the only intact example of an X-Craft is at the Royal Navy Submarine Museum, Gosport.

14

Ghostly Scotland

'To a Scot, the past clings like sand to wet feet,
and is carried about as a burden.

The many ghosts are always a part of them, inescapable.'

Geddes MacGregor,
Edinburgh-educated author and academic

The Scots love a ghost, and with the long nights, dark history
and ancient folklore it's perhaps little wonder this country enjoys
a reputation as one of the most haunted on the globe. No list
can hope even to be representative, let alone complete, but the
following gives some idea of what might be keeping locals and
visitors alike awake.

A75 between Annan and Dumfries

Drivers on a stretch of main road approximately a dozen miles
long have on several occasions reported seeing terrifying apparitions that vanish moments before being struck by vehicles using
the road. The apparitions have never been identified or explained,

although popular suggestions include the ghosts of those killed on the road either by local bandits or in a road traffic accident. Witnesses to the apparitions also refer to a sudden drop in temperature as they approach the site.

A84 Lochearnhead to Balquhidder

A ghost train – all lights lit but no one on board – has been observed by visitors on the Lochearnhead to Balquhidder road, even though the nearest railway line was closed by a landslide back in 1965.

Ackergill Tower, near Wick, Caithness

Now run as a hotel and conference venue, this remote outpost of Caithness has seen visitors report sightings of the ghost of the raven-haired Helen Gunn. She is said to have been kidnapped by members of the Keith family, then owners of the castle, as part of a long-running feud with her own family and that of the Sinclairs. Locked in one of the highest rooms in the tower, she jumped or fell to her death, and continues to return from time to time to scare the present occupants.

Airth Castle, Stirlingshire

Guests at this hotel overlooking the Forth River have reported seeing the ghosts of a woman, possibly a nanny, with two young children who are said to have died in a fire before the castle was converted. It is said that the children can be heard playing happily in several of the rooms, but guests and staff have also heard cries and screams. A spectral dog is also believed to roam the corridors, and to snap at the ankles of anyone passing.

Ardrossan Castle, Ayrshire

The atmospheric ruins – the castle was destroyed on Cromwell's orders – are believed by many to be haunted by the ghost of William Wallace, returned from London where he was hanged, drawn and quartered in 1305. He is said to walk the ramparts on stormy nights, while a second ghost is that of Sir Fergus Barclay, the so-called Devil of Ardrossan whose remarkable horsemanship is attributed to a pact he made with Beelzebub in exchange for a magic bridle.

Auchen Castle, Dumfries and Galloway

Not to be confused with the 19th-century replacement (now a hotel), Auchen's ruins dating back to 1220 are haunted by the vaguely translucent ghost of a child who stalks the remains during the hours after midnight.

Baldoon Castle, Galloway

Another ruin, but the seat of the Dunbars of Westfield from around 1530 to the 1800s, and the setting for the bloody tale of Baldoon that inspired Sir Walter Scott's *Bride of Lammermuir*. Forced to marry against her will, Janet Dalrymple went mad and stabbed her husband on their wedding night in the 1660s, or perhaps she killed him first and was afterwards declared insane. Either way, she is now said to roam the castle dressed in a blood-spattered wedding gown.

Ben Macdui, Cairngorms

On this remote mountain landscape, Britain's second highest peak at 4,296 feet, walkers and others have reported an exceptionally tall grey phantom with indistinct features. Known to Gaelic speakers as *An Fear Liath Mor*, the creature has been described as a kind of yeti and as the guardian of an inter-dimensional portal, but it could just as easily be a trick of the light.

Borthwick Castle, Lothian

It was from the besieged 15th-century Borthwick Castle that Mary, Queen of Scots, escaped disguised as a pageboy after her third marriage in 1567 to the 4th Earl of Bothwell. Her ghost is occasionally seen here now dressed as a boy (but hopefully not by the happy couples who book the castle for their own weddings).

Brigadoon, Highlands

The idea of ghost village which appears once every 100 years is now a popular Scottish myth, although the original was wholly German. The story of Germelshausen is what inspired composers Alan Jay Lerner and Frederick Loewe, but in 1947 filming in war-ravaged Germany would not have been possible. Because of this they decided to reset the tale in Scotland, perhaps inspired by the medieval Brig o'Doon in the Robert Burns poem 'Tam o' Shanter'. Unfortunately Scotland's inclement weather did for that idea, so it was filmed entirely in California. This, however, has not prevented visitors here from stopping at tourist offices to ask when and where the village is next set to appear.

Brodick Castle, Isle of Arran

Captured and largely destroyed by the English during the Wars of Independence, the castle was rebuilt and strengthened when it was occupied by Cromwell in the 17th century. Ghosts include that of a young lady who starved to death in the dungeons after being diagnosed with the plague, and a white stag that frequents the grounds whenever a chief of the Hamilton clan is close to death.

Castle Fraser, Aberdeenshire

Now run by the National Trust for Scotland, Castle Fraser was held by the family of that name for almost 500 years. In the 19th century a young woman, her identity still a mystery although some say she was a princess, was dragged downstairs by her hair and murdered. Her ghost has never been seen but stains, presumed to be blood, are said occasionally to manifest themselves on the stone stairs. Unfortunately the latter have since been covered in wood, making the story hard to verify. Trust staff have also reported hearing piano music when no one is playing the piano and laughter from empty rooms; the ghost of Lady Blanche Drummond (1848–74), first wife of Lt Col. Frederick Mackenzie Fraser, has appeared in a long black gown in the castle grounds and on the main staircase.

Castle of Mey

Likely to be the last castle to join the royal fold – the estate was acquired by the queen mother as recently as 1952 and is now preserved as part of a charitable trust – this remote corner of Caithness is haunted by the ghost of Lady Fanny Sinclair. The daughter of the 14th Earl of Caithness (1821–81) eloped with a servant and, after being brought back to the castle against her will, was locked in a bedroom in one of the towers. So far so fairy-tale, but in October 1883 she leapt to her death and is said to haunt the bedroom to this day.

Craigievar Castle, Aberdeenshire

Enchanting Craigievar Castle was completed by the Forbes family in 1626. It is haunted by a member of the Gordon family said to have been forced at the point of a blade to jump from a fourth-floor window by Sir John Forbes to prevent him marrying the daughter of the house. A second ghost, of a fiddler, is only ever seen by members of the Forbes clan.

Crathes Castle, Aberdeenshire

At another property owned by the National Trust for Scotland, the Green Lady's Room is haunted by the restless spirit of a young woman carrying a child. Although her identity is not known she is thought to have been made pregnant by a servant, and reportedly disappeared after the servant was dismissed. Years later workmen renovating the castle uncovered two skeletons beneath one of the fireplaces.

Culcreuch Castle, Stirlingshire

Situated near the banks of Loch Lomond, this 13th-century tower house is haunted by a harpist. After being wounded in a skirmish in 1582, a young man was brought back to the castle to die. To console herself his mistress took up the *clarsach*, a wire-stringed instrument, and she can still be heard, particularly in the dead of night.

Culzean Castle, Ayrshire

The former home of the former home of the Marquesses of Ailsa, chiefs of Clan Kennedy, Culzean is home to at least seven ghosts, including a phantom piper. Sadly, US president Dwight D. Eisenhower's is not among them, although he spent considerable time staying in the castle, having been gifted an apartment here in recognition of his important role as Supreme Commander of the Allied Forces in Europe during the Second World War.

Dalzell House, North Lanarkshire

The three different ladies – known as Green, Grey and White – said to haunt Dalzell relate to three different eras, and have been observed by guests and guards. Dogs too occasionally become spooked when walking into apparently empty rooms. Inevitably, one of the three is said to have jumped to her death, but the Grey Lady is perhaps the more unusual, with those who have seen her describing a nurse from the Great War, when the house was commandeered for use as a hospital for wounded soldiers.

Dryburgh Abbey Hotel, Borders

A hotel since the 1930s, Dryburgh has its own Grey Lady, believed to be the ghost of a young lady who drowned herself in the Tweed fearing a scandal after the murder of her lover, who was a monk at the nearby abbey.

Dunstaffnage Castle, Oban

Fortified, according to legend, since the 1st century BC, the present castle dates from the 13th century and was long held by the Clan Campbell as a raiding point against the MacDonalds and Macleans. A 16th-century Cameron of Lochiel was beheaded here, and in 1746 Flora MacDonald was imprisoned in the castle after helping Prince Charles Edward Stewart escape to France. The identity of the ghost is neither of these, however, but, dressed in green and known as the 'Ell-maid of Dunstaffnage', its appearances are said to foreshadow any major event, good or ill, about to befall the Hereditary Keeper of the Castle (see Ceremonial Scotland).

Edinburgh Castle, Lothian

With a long history and the closest associations with Scotland's story, Edinburgh Castle is said to be the most haunted in the country, with two musicians among its more interesting ghouls. One is a piper who was sent into the network of tunnels that underlie the castle. He was never seen again, although his pipes are sometimes heard. The sound of drums is also said to be discernible ahead of any attacks on the castle, although no assault has been mounted for many years.

High Street, Edinburgh

A spectral piper is said to play in a secret tunnel underlying the street, close to the Heart of Midlothian, where tradition dictates passers-by should spit on the site of an ancient gaol at which the heads of traitors and others were displayed on iron spikes.

Fyvie Castle, Aberdeenshire

In the 1920s workmen engaged in restoring the castle found the skeleton of a woman behind a bedroom wall. Following the respectful burial of her remains, the family living in the castle began to experience a number of unexplained occurrences and strange sounds. In response, the head of the family decided to have the remains disinterred and returned to the bedroom, after which the haunting reportedly stopped. The castle also has a recurring, indelible stain, much like the one in Oscar Wilde's *The Canterville Ghost*, and its own 'Green Lady' (see Pinkie House, below).

Glamis Castle, Angus

The ancestral home of Queen Elizabeth, George VI's widow, and the birthplace of HRH Princess Margaret, the castle is haunted by the ghost of a 'Grey Lady' who was burned at the stake after being accused of witchcraft by James V. One room is also haunted by the 4th Earl of Crawford, aka 'Earl Beardie', who is said to have used it to play cards with the devil in the mid-15th century. (Curiously, this same legend is associated with Lordscairnie Castle in Fife, even though this was built after his death by his heir, the 1st Duke of Montrose.)

Greyfriars Kirkyard, Edinburgh

The churchyard is haunted by the ghost of George Mackenzie, a 17th-century lawyer known as 'Bluidy Mackenzie' for his vigorous and cold-hearted pursuit and torture of members of the Presbyterian Covenanters movement. Unusually, the hauntings began only in the 1990s, reportedly after a tramp had broken into MacKenzie tomb, since when scores of visitors have said they were attacked while walking in the grounds, with many more collapsing. More recently an attempt was made at exorcising the site, but this failed and the exorcist died shortly afterwards.

Holyrood Palace, Edinburgh

A naked phantom known as Bald Agnes is said to roam the palace. This is believed to be the ghost of Agnes Sampson from Nether Keith who, after being interrogated personally by James VI, was stripped naked, tortured, garrotted and then burned for witchcraft in 1590. (More on this in the Witchy Scotland chapter.)

Huntingtower Castle, Perthshire

An unusual example of a happy, helpful ghost, 'Milady Greensleeves' is occasionally seen in advance of a death, but more than once has been said to have cured sick people staying in the castle.

Inveraray Castle, Argyll

The picturesque seat and ancestral home of the Dukes of Argyll is mostly 18th-century, with later additions by the architect of London's Paddington Station. Devastated by fire in the 1970s, and now restored and open to the public, it is reportedly haunted by the ghost of another harpist who was executed in 1644 after spying on the – presumably naked – lady of the house. Visitors claim to have heard the plaintive sound of his playing, the present duchess insisting that one bedroom in particular (formerly belonging to Queen Victoria's fourth daughter who married the 9th Duke) is 'riddled with ghosts'.

Iona

Many visitors to Iona experience a somehow mysterious peace and sense of tranquility, but in the 1940s a clergyman visiting the island claimed to have seen Scotland's strangest phantom, namely the whole of the old 7th-century abbey. As this was in ruins by the 1700s it seems unlikely, but similar 'time-slips' have been reported since, together with sightings of Viking longboats waiting offshore to raid the holy island.

Jedburgh Castle, Borders

In the old county of Roxburghshire, Jedburgh is home to several ghosts, including a spectral piper who wanders the battlements, and a number of mysterious lights. Recent visitors to the nearby gaol, now a youth hostel, have also reported feeling the occasional presence of paranormal activity.

Leith Hall, Aberdeenshire

During a drunken brawl in Aberdeen on Christmas Day 1763, the laird, John Leith III, was shot in the head and died. His ghost, arrayed in dark green Highland dress with a bloodstained bandage covering his eyes, is said to walk the corridors of his former home, crying in pain, and on occasion this has badly scared guests staying at the house.

Lewis, Western Isles

More sea spirits than ghosts, the Blue Men of Minch are a cave-dwelling race said to inhabit the straits between the island and the mainland. Humanlike but with blue skin, its members are said to swim alongside fishing boats while trying to lure sailors into the sea, or conjure up storms to wreck the boats.

Mary King's Close, Edinburgh

Although evidence for this celebrated Old Town massacre is hard to come by, local legend insists the close is haunted by the ghosts of plague victims who were herded into the area on the orders of the authorities and left to starve. A reputation as Scotland's most haunted street has given it a major boost as a tourist attraction.

Pinkie House, Lothian

This largely 16th-century Musselburgh tower house is now a school, but was once the seat of the abbots of Dunfermline. It occupies the site of the Battle of Pinkie Cleagh (1547), the last pitched battle between the English and Scottish armies, which ended in a catastrophic defeat for the Scots. One might assume that any local hauntings would relate to a day still known as 'Black Saturday', but in fact the ghost is that of a young woman, Lilias Drummond. Occasionally seen with a child, she was the wife of Alexander Seton, James VI's chancellor and the 1st Earl of Dunfermline, and as the 'Green Lady' is also said to haunt Fyvie Castle.

River Meldrum

The Den, an area of river bank close to Cortachy Castle in Angus, the family seat of the late Sir Angus Ogilvy, is haunted by a 'thing' that brings terror to anyone who looks upon it. Fortunately, anyone in love is said to be immune to its power, so Sir Angus and his wife HRH Princess Alexandra claimed never to have felt its effect.

RAF Montrose, Angus

In 1910 the Hon. Charles Stewart Rolls, co-founder of the famous motor car company, became the first Briton to die in an air crash.

Scotland's first fatality came three years later, a young Irishman, Lt Desmond Arthur of the Royal Flying Corps, who crashed when his B.E.2 205 biplane collapsed during a routine training flight from Upper Dysart to Lunan Bay. His body was flung clear of the wreckage, but with almost every bone in his body broken he died immediately.

The first sighting of Arthur's ghost was made less than a year later, when a figure answering his description strolled into the officers' mess. Many others followed during the course of the Great War, but were frequently not reported by young men anxious not to be thought mad. For a few years after the war nothing else happened, but then in 1940 a Hurricane pilot was said to have been distracted by the sight of a biplane lifting off the runway. Sightings continued until the base was closed a decade later, with the most remarkable a few years after that when another pilot, this time flying a civilian aircraft, reported seeing a biplane similar to Arthur's plummet to the ground. The airfield is these days non-operational but open to the public as the Montrose Air Station Heritage Centre.

Stirling Castle, Stirling

The castle is home to two spectral females, a 'Pink Lady' sometimes said to be the ghost of Mary, Queen of Scots, and a 'Green Lady' believed to be the ghost of one of her servants. The latter is reported to have saved the life of the queen, but lost her own after extinguishing a fire in the sovereign's bedroom. A third spectre, the traditionally dressed 'Highland Ghost', has been observed on many occasions by visitors and was even photographed in 1935 by an architect working on the building's restoration.

15

Witch-crazed Scotland

'One sort of such said to be witches, are women which be commonly old, lame, poor, sullen, superstitious. They are leane and deformed, shewing melancholie in their faces, to the horror of all that see them.'

Reginald Scot,
The Discoverie of Witchcraft (1584)

The very last nation in Europe to repeal its anti-witchcraft legislation, the last publicly to execute a person for the crime of witchcraft, and the last to have one of its countrymen prosecuted for witchcraft (this was as recently as 1944), no one else has pursued witches with the ferocity, zeal and determination of the Scots. Particularly during a period of around 200 years, during the 16th and 17th centuries, the country went through something of a dark age, a time of fear and panic that saw literally thousands of innocent men and women persecuted on the basis of the flimsiest evidence and thrown to the flames.

A Timeline of Scottish Witchcraft

1479: John Stewart, 1st Earl of Mar and Garloch, died in mysterious circumstances, possibly executed for employing witches to kill his brother, James III.

1537: Janet Douglas, Lady Glamis, was accused of treason and witchcraft by James V personally. After being tortured in the dungeons of Edinburgh Castle, and eventually confessing under extreme duress, she was burned to death on the castle esplanade in the presence of her young son.

1563: A new Witchcraft Act came in for Scotland, Mary, Queen of Scots, seeking specifically to ensure that no person should 'use any manner of witchcraft, sorcery or necromancy, nor give themselves forth to have any such craft or knowledge thereof'. Witch prickers were widely employed to prick or 'brodd' the body of anyone accused of witchcraft. If the person didn't bleed this was used as evidence to haul them up in court, with burning alive as the preferred and so routine punishment.

(In England, meanwhile, execution was by hanging, but only when witchcraft was used to kill; lesser spells called for no more than time spent in the pillory. Also, because English law at this time did not allow torture as part of an investigation, witch hunts were smaller in scale and usually less brutal.)

1576: In a rare case involving a coven, Bessie Dunlop of Lynne was burned on Castle Hill, Edinburgh. She had been found guilty of consorting with a group of eight women witches and four men, and of receiving herbs from the Queen of the Faeries. (Such groups were only occasionally 'revealed' under torture, typically numbering from two to ten individuals, although one case mentioned 2,400.)

1590: A record year for persecutions in Scotland, following the loss of a ship travelling with James VI back from Denmark.

The disaster was attributed to bad weather called down on the fleet by witches (possibly operating from North Berwickshire), after which the outraged sovereign declared that all witches, all ages, all ranks 'and even bairns' should now be put to death by fire. Under torture many in the area confessed to having met with the devil, with some being interrogated at Holyrood by the king himself.

1591: Records from this time put the cost of executing a witch in the capital – by garotte and burning – at £6 8s 10d (£6.45). *Newes from Scotland*, a popular illustrated pamphlet published the same year, described in detail some of the tortures to which the accused could look forward, but their use was actually quite unusual. Sleep deprivation and starvation were usually enough to obtain a false confession, although in special cases fingernails were pulled out, pins driven into flesh and legs confined in hollow tubes before wedges of wood were hammered in to shatter the bones and cause the marrow to ooze.

1591: Alice Sampson, the so-called wise wife of Keith, worked as a midwife and healer in East Lothian until she was accused of witchcraft by one of her rivals, a woman called Duncan. Refusing to confess, 'she was taken and brought to Haliruid House before the Kings Maiestie ... where she was straitly examined'. Examination here meant being subjected to some not inconsiderable torture, after which she immediately agreed that she was indeed responsible for 'sundrye thinges which were so miraculous and strange' and had celebrated a black mass with up to 200 other witches. For this she was garrotted and then burnt at the stake at Edinburgh's Castlehill.

1594: The islands were no safer than the mainland, and in Orkney Alesoun (or Alison) Balfour of Stenness was implicated in a murder plot and named as a 'known notorious witch'. Taken to Kirkwall Castle and tortured, her legs were put into the caschielawis (see Gruesome Scotland chapter for more details), but after forty-eight hours she said nothing. Her husband and two children were then brought before her, the former placed in lang irons – a device designed to crush its victim – and crushed beneath 700 lb of stones. Again she said nothing, nor when her son's legs were broken with scores of hammer blows. Only when her seven-year-old daughter was put in thumbscrews did she decide to speak, confessing to witchcraft after most of the girl's fingers had been broken. On 15 December she was put to death.

1596: Aberdeen, too, proved itself particularly adept at tracking down scores of suspects, with anyone accused of 'witchcraft, sorcery and other diabolical and detestable practices' quickly finding themselves before the Provost of Aberdeen, four baillies and a jury at the city's Tolbooth. Dittays – the name given to the lists of charges – could go back literally decades, and frequently relied on accusations from neighbours and even family members.

1596: The same year John Leyis and his three daughters, Elspet, Janet and Violet, were also accused of sorcery by the Aberdeen authorities. Fortunately they were cleared on all counts of witchcraft but found guilty of being in the company of witches and acting as their accomplices. For this they were banished from the city and the surrounding area and thereafter forbidden to come within ten miles of the burgh.

1597: Scotland's second great witch hunt took place when Margaret Aitken, the so-called Great Witch of Balwearie, generously offered to identify other witches in exchange for her life. For several months she travelled the country ratting out strangers, before her expertise was called into question when she pointed the finger at several people she had previously cleared. Unfortunately by this time as many as 400 had already been put on trial for witchcraft and other diabolical crimes, and perhaps 200 of them executed.

1597: The same year James VI offered up a theory as to 'the cause that there are twentie women given to that craft, where ther is one man'. The reason he thought pretty straightforward: 'for as that sexe is frailer than men is, so it is easier to be intrapped in these grosse snares of the Devil, as was over will proved to be true, by the Serpent's deceiving of Eva at the beginning, which makes him the homlier with that sexe sensine.'

1598: While a majority of those accused were indeed women (in excess of 80%), men were by no means safe from persecution. Thomas Ego, for example, was charged with using witchcraft and sorcery, declared a fugitive from justice and in his absence had all his belongings confiscated.

1603: On becoming king of England (as James I) the Scottish monarch denied having been instrumental in pursuing so vigorously the subject of Scottish witchcraft. This was despite his earlier publication of *Daemonologie*, an eighty-page book in which he expounded his own views on the topic in an attempt to encourage intellectual debate around the subject of witchcraft, and the passing less than a year later of a new Witchcraft Act.

1605 (or thereabouts): Three very famous Scottish witches – the weird or 'weyward' sisters – made their debut appearance in William Shakespeare's *Macbeth*. At a time when witchcraft was very much in the news a publication such as the king's *Daemonologie* would have been familiar to a well-read man like Shakespeare, but the trio may also have been inspired by the *Chronicles* of Raphael Holinshed (1529–1580). In this work a future king of Scotland encounters 'three women in strange and wild apparell, resembling creatures of elder world'.

1614: In a particularly gruesome case an Edinburgh man called Robert Erskine, together with his sisters Annas and Issobell, was beheaded at Mercat Cross after being found guilty of consulting with witches and 'poisoning and treasonable murder'.

1625: The death of James VI brought no let-up in the number of persecutions. The reasons for this continue to be debated, but historians point to the inarguable fact that 17th-century Scotland was a country still very much in the zealous grip of the Presbyterian Reformation. As such, it was a place where theologians were keen to ditch one established Catholic icon, that of femininity represented by the Virgin Mary, in favour of another, namely Eve the fallen woman. In such a climate, with the Kirk and the judiciary working closely together, women all too often found themselves caught in the sights of the witch-hunters.

1629: Records show the son of the official executioner at Peebles was paid twelve shillings (60p) to act as dempster at the execution of three more witches. This required him to pronounce the sentence and, in the event of the executioner being unable to complete his task, to carry it out himself. The executioner would have earned as much as £10, equivalent to what a successful Edinburgh tradesman might have expected to make in a year.

1636: Margaret Fraser, an Aberdeen woman suspected of witchcraft, managed to escape from her place of detention, but such was the enthusiasm of her accusers that she was still being sought fifteen years later when, presumably to their dismay, it was reported that she had died of natural causes.

1649: More than 600 surviving records attest to yet another golden age for witch hunts north of the border, suggesting that nearly 300 of those accused were executed. Most went before fairly *ad hoc* courts, often presided over by local clerics or landowners who as often as not would lean on the accused to name others in the area who might be guilty of similar offences. This ensured that further suspects were never in short supply, but occasionally justice was done, as in the case of a Dunfermline brewer who in February of this year was able to defend himself against a charge of using magic to improve the quality of his beer.

1650: Witch-fever briefly spilled over the border into Newcastle upon Tyne and Berwick-upon-Tweed, where similar trials took place. It is interesting to note, however, that in both places (and in several small villages in Northumberland) it was generally the case that itinerant Scottish witch hunters were involved in whipping up local hysteria.

1661–62: Scotland's final great witch hunt saw hundreds more witch trials over a period of about sixteen months. In all more than 650 people were tried, mostly women, and mostly low to middling status. The hunt started in April in Midlothian and East Lothian, where 206 people were accused of sorcery of some sort or another. Thereafter it rapidly spread across the country, although the precise number of executions is unknown because so many different courts were involved.

1662: Christian Caddell disguised herself as 'John Dickson' to become Scotland's only female witch pricker. Engaged in the search for the devil's mark, that spot on the body where a pin could be slipped in without the accused bleeding or feeling any pain, she had her victims stripped naked and then shaved from head to toe. Such was the humiliation of this that many would confess just to make her stop, but Caddell was too keen to fall for this, receiving six shillings a day maintenance (30p) while she was working, and £6 a head for every witch she nabbed.

1663: Eventually found out, Caddell narrowly avoided a charge of witchcraft herself, but was sentenced to exile in the West Indies. She was transported to Barbados, a considerable punishment at a time when many settlers died of horrible tropical diseases, and left Forres on 4 May. This was the very day that one of the last 'witches' she had identified was executed, one of at least six and perhaps as many as ten innocent lives that were lost due to Caddell's machinations and greed.

1670: After confessing to 'supernatural intelligence' relating to the Scottish defeat at the Battle of Worcester twenty years earlier, Thomas Weir was locked up in an old leper colony at Greenside beneath Edinburgh's Calton Hill. A distinguished former soldier, his confessions were at first ignored until they became so wild and treasonous the authorities were forced to take action. Eventually they decided to garrotte and burn him at the Gallowlee on the Leith road. His sister, with whom he had publicly confessed to enjoying an incestuous relationship, was afterwards burned at Grassmarket.

1692: The most famous witch trials of them all – in Salem, Massachusetts – illustrate how the pursuit of witches now stretched far beyond Scotland. Even here, however, the dead hand of James VI could be detected, the implications of his 1604 Witchcraft Act and Britain's rapid colonisation of the eastern seaboard of the American continent having provided the perfect means of spreading the fear.

1697: Margaret Lang, John Lindsay, James Lindsay, John Reid, Catherine Campbell, Margaret Fulton and Agnes Naismith – collectively known as the Paisley Witches – were condemned to hang and then burn on Gallow Green for tormenting and bewitching the eleven-year-old daughter of the Laird of Bargarran. The last mass execution of witches saw six of them swing, a seventh having killed himself in advance. A curse supposedly voiced by one of the six was for years afterwards blamed for every ill that befell the town until Christian Shaw, the eleven-year-old in question, finally admitted the whole thing was a hoax.

1698: Executioners were well paid for this sort of thing but also so widely reviled that one of them, William Kirk, the executioner in a case in Kirkcudbright, could find nowhere to stay in the town and was forced to live in the local prison.

1704: The year saw the last case on record of a Scottish subject being tortured on a charge of witchcraft although the Privy

Council had sought several years previously to ensure that torture was used only with its express permission. The celebrated ducking stool was almost never used, however, and possibly not used at all after 1597, as the idea that witches could float had long since been discredited.

1705: In Fife Janet Cornfoot, the so-called Witch of Pittenweem, was accused of bewitching the local blacksmith's apprentice, and after being flogged by the local minister was locked in the town's tollbooth. Managing to escape, she was recaptured by a mob, dragged down to the beach and, after being beaten up and pelted with rocks, left for dead beneath a door weighed down by heavy stones and trampled by horses. Some 300 years later the townspeople were offered the chance to put up a memorial to the murdered woman, but they decide not to bother.

1720: The twelve-year-old son of James, 7th Lord Torphichen, claimed he had been bewitched by an old woman in Calder. Afterwards he reportedly fell into a trance 'from which no horse-whipping could rouse him till he chose his own time to revive', and could float above the ground. Five locals were arrested and flung into jail, but by the time they came to trial so much time had elapsed that they were merely publicly rebuked and allowed to go free.

1727: Janet Horne became the last person to be publicly executed as a witch in Scotland. Accused by her neighbours of riding to the devil on her daughter's back, and unable to repeat (in Gaelic) the Lord's Prayer at her trial, she was put to death in Carnaig Street in the Littletown area of Dornoch. Her body was burned to ashes in a wooden barrel filled with flaming tar.

While accurate numbers are hard to obtain, a survey of 305 Scottish witchcraft cases – approximately 10% of the total – shows that 205 were executed, 52 acquitted, 27 banished, 11 lost (i.e. declared fugitive), 6 excommunicated, 2 'put to the horn'

– meaning outlawed – and one person was kept in prison with another ordered to be publicly humiliated.

1736: Scotland's Witchcraft Act is finally repealed, a year after the British Parliament moved to scrap a broadly similar piece of English legislation. The crime of witchcraft was henceforth abolished and replaced by a new crime of 'pretended witchcraft', carrying a relatively modest maximum penalty of one year's imprisonment. Interestingly, during the 173-year life of the Act not a single witch had been accused of using a broomstick for anything but sweeping up, and there are only nine cases on record of a witch being said to have a 'familiar' such as a black cat.

1886: Following publication of the haunting novella *The Strange Case of Dr Jekyll and Mr Hyde*, interest in the aforementioned Thomas Weir is revived amidst rumours that it was he who provided the inspiration for Robert Louis Stevenson's memorably evil character.

1944: In a fascinating footnote Helen Duncan, a middle-aged medium from Callander in Perthshire, becomes the last person to be jailed under the 1735 Witchcraft Act, after claiming to have conjured up the spirit of a sailor killed when HMS *Barham* had gone down three years earlier. To maintain national morale the ship's loss to a German U-boat had been kept secret and, fearful that she might reveal details of the forthcoming D-Day landings as well, the authorities took immediate action.

She was found guilty of 'pretending to raise spirits from the dead'. This was a convenient clause someone managed to unearth from the 18th-century statute, and she was promptly sentenced to nine months in HMP Holloway in north London. Although it had proved useful in wartime, in 1951 the laughably antiquated legislation was finally scrapped in favour of a new and more appropriate Fraudulent Mediums Act.

16

Criminal Scotland

'The first thing we do, let's kill all the lawyers.'

William Shakespeare, *Henry VI, Part II*

The Law Really is an Ass

Although the 15th-century statute banning golf has been rescinded (see Sporting chapter), a number of ancient laws pertaining to Scotland and the Scottish are still in force, or so commonly thought to be that they may as well be. Needless to say, prosecutions for most are non-existent these days, and even in the past were so rare that it is tempting to suppose that such regulations were brought in only to assist authors of books such as this one.

- A Scotsman can be shot in York if he's carrying a bow and arrow. Much the same is said of Berwick-on-Tweed and Carlisle, the obvious conclusion being that local by-laws were introduced at a time when cross-border incursions were less welcome than they are now.
- It is illegal for a boy under the age of ten to see a naked mannequin. It's not really been made clear whether the child

commits the offence by peeping, or the retailer for arranging for such a lewd display, and anyway this one sounds almost impossible to police.

- Scottish homeowners are obliged to allow anyone knocking at their door to use the loo. For centuries trespass was an offence in England but not in Scotland, but this seems to be taking the spirit of Highland hospitality a bit far even so.

- Whales washed up on the shore belong to the sovereign. There is some substance to this – the whalebone traditionally went to the queen for her corsets, and the blubber was valuable for its oil – although it's been a long time since any monarch insisted on claiming the prize.

- It is illegal to be drunk in charge of a cow. Under the terms of the Licensing Act (1872), drunks can still be jailed and fined up to £200 if caught in charge of a steam engine or 'propelling' a horse or cow that is being used as a draught animal on the public highway.

- It is illegal to sexually assault a drinks trolley. There is no specific statute for this, but as recently as 2013 a rail passenger travelling on the Aberdeen–Glasgow service was charged with a criminal offence after propositioning and then manhandling a catering trolley in a lewd fashion. In recent years other Scots have found themselves in court over similar attempts to get to know traffic cones, shoes, a frozen chicken and a stretch of pavement.

'PRISON WAS A HOLIDAY CAMP'

With Scotland having some of the toughest gaols anywhere in Britain not everyone welcomes the chance to spend time behind bars, but one man who did, German stormtrooper Heinrich Steinmeyer, said years later he planned to leave his life savings of around £430,000 to pensioners in Perthshire. The reason, he said, was a kind of thank-you, because after being captured in Normandy in 1944 he had really enjoyed his time at Cultybraggan prisoner-of-war camp near Comrie. Believing the Scots Guards platoon that took him prisoner had prevented a group of local French women from killing him, the former Waffen SS officer found himself sent to Perthshire, where the camp guards and local villagers treated him so well that he decided to stay in Scotland for a further seven years after the war had ended.

It's Not Just Shops Down South Who Reject the Scottish Pound

When the so-called Great Train Robbers knocked off the Glasgow-to-Euston express in 1963, gang members foolishly ditched hundreds of Scottish pound notes because, as naïve working-class Londoners, they didn't want anything to do with dodgy foreign currency. Their ignorance cost them dear, as police found incriminating fingerprints at the gang's hide-out, where they had used the money to play Monopoly. In fact, this was only one of several elementary mistakes made by the supposed master criminals, and following the £2.6 million heist the chief getaway driver Roy John James was caught red-handed with several stolen fivers, which were immediately traced back to the National Commercial Bank in Inverness.

The Kidd Who Couldn't Help It?

Scotland's most notorious pirate, Greenock-born Captain William Kidd (1645–1701), tried going straight, but apparently couldn't hack it. Fêted by the authorities after shrewdly targeting

French ships only, he married well and received a bounty of £150 after successfully hunting down 'pirates, freebooters and sea-rovers of whatever nature soever'. Unfortunately around 1699 he appears to have gone back over to the dark side. After shooting dead a crewmember who threatened to mutiny he was found guilty of murder and five indictments of piracy. The judgment divided public opinion down the middle, and the Admiralty is still thought to have suppressed evidence that might have cleared him. He was nevertheless hanged at the riverside Execution Dock in east London, perhaps to rid the authorities of someone who had become an embarrassment. As was often the case, the execution was badly bungled: the rope broke the first time, and a clearly drunk Kidd fell to the ground before being strung up once again. Slowly strangled, the body was then left in chains for three tides to wash over it.

Scotland: A Paradise for Smugglers

With differential tax rates across the border before the Union, and even greater discrepancies after it, smuggling has a very long history in Scotland and is perhaps the country's most colourful crime. Historically, whisky accounted for much of the contraband, but particularly in the 17th and 18th centuries smuggling Virginia tobacco, French brandy, gin, tea, salt and even Irish oatmeal provided literally thousands of Scots with employment – and an opportunity to thumb their noses at the establishment and the English.

- Traditionally, illegal distilling occurred most commonly in the glens, where practitioners could find an abundance of fresh water to soak the barley grains and hiding places to conceal their kit. Excise men or gaugers knew to look for telltale smoke from peat fires (used to heat the stills), but with such huge areas to search always missed more than they found.

- In 1778 Edinburgh had eight legal stills and an estimated 400 where the owners paid no duty, although the distilling itself was not illegal. After 1814, however, a new law effectively banned private distilling altogether by outlawing the operation of any still with a capacity of less than 500 gallons.

- Then as now a high proportion of Scottish moonshine was obviously drunk locally, but much of it was exported to England. The most ingenious way of doing this was by using what were known as belly canteens, stout metal containers that could be strapped onto a woman to give the impression that she was pregnant. Other much larger vessels incorporated fake heads, and when positioned behind a horseman's saddle looked from a distance like a second person riding pillion.

- Church ministers, like the Reverend Andrew Burns from Glen Isla, frequently found themselves on the side of their community rather than the tax collectors, and would tip off the locals whenever the enforcers were known to be on their way.

- His namesake, the poet Robbie Burns, trained as a gauger while farming near Dumfries. From 1788 until his death in 1796 he was employed catching smugglers, at one stage earning a handsome £50 a year, until this was reduced to £35 as his health declined.

- Another great penman, Sir Walter Scott, maintained that 'few people take more enthusiastically to the "free-trade" than the men of the Solway coast'. He modelled Dirk Hatteraick in *Guy Mannering* on one of the practitioners in the area patrolled by Burns, where villages such as Annan Waterfoot, Borgue, Kenziels and Ruthwell were frequently associated with illegal derring-do.

- Certainly at times it must have looked as though the crime was getting out of hand, with what one observer described as 'the insolence and audacity of the smugglers' matched only by their brazenness as they 'ride openly thro the country . . . in troops of 20, 30, 40 and sometimes upwards 50 horses suffering no officer to come near to try to discover who they are, far less to seize their goods'.

- Many old cottages around the coast had room to hide a barrel or two, but at Eyemouth in East Berwickshire the immense Gunsgreen House was built above the harbour with the express intention of thwarting the gaugers. Designed in 1753 by John Adam, a member of the famous architectural dynasty, the large stone mansion was a veritable cabinet of criminality. With large cellars linked directly to the sea, and a bespoke 'tea chute' for hiding the precious commodity, it even had a fireplace that, 'by moving some knob or lever, could swing out of its place like a gate being opened', providing a hidden doorway to a secret passage. So many living in the town were engaged in similar illegal activities (albeit on a smaller scale than Gunsgreen's owner) that for a long time there was said to be more Eyemouth below ground than above it.

- Goods from Ireland most commonly found their way to Glasgow and Kilmarnock by way of Ayr, and included shipments of that alien stuff, Irish whiskey. This was known locally as 'Arran Water', and despite modern Scots' dismissal of anything but the genuine article it was a huge earner for those bringing it in under cover of darkness.

- Occasionally smugglers were caught, and in 1792 several of them were imprisoned at Campbeltown on the Kintyre peninsula. One spent a full four days cutting a hole through the floor of his cell, but when finally he dropped through it he realised he had burrowed his way into the local courthouse.

- Further south in the Cheviots a path called Sauter's Road near Pathhead is a reminder of the thriving trade smuggling Irish salt through Scotland to English markets. (Sauter's Ford on the River Ale in Roxburghshire has similar origins.)

- Some indication of the value of all this can be discerned from the lengths to which people went to get their hands on contraband. In the town of Montrose in 1734 a gang of smugglers retrieved sixty ankers of brandy – about 500 gallons – by breaking into a shipbuilder's and tunnelling down into the cellar and then through the wall of the adjacent property. The barrels were then rolled through the shipbuilder's house and out into the street, which he failed to notice, having presumably being handsomely paid to turn a blind eye.

- For a long while smuggling was estimated to be the second largest industry in the city of Aberdeen (after whaling) and, charged with patrolling more than seventy miles of coast, the gaugers simply couldn't cope. On one stretch towards Peterhead an estimated 8,000 gallons of European spirits were being landed every month, and in 1721 the contraband listed as seized included not just brandy, oil and an incredible 3,000 lb of tobacco but also raisins, figs and even prunes.

- Further north the situation was little better, and for two or three years in the late 1790s the Shetlands almost ran out of money because so much currency was being sent to Scandinavia in exchange for illegal shipments of gin. Thereafter things slowly improved, but only because, having 'drained the poor of this country ... of every shilling they could spare or raise', the smugglers found themselves going out of business because no one could afford to buy what they had to sell.

TOO GOOD TO BE TROON

In 2014 a survey suggested that Scots were less likely to buy counterfeit goods than English, Welsh and especially Northern Irish consumers, but that hasn't stopped the country producing its fair share of fraudsters and fakers – nor indeed of gulls.

Scotsman **Arthur Furguson** (1883–1938) is popularly supposed to have sold various bits of London to American tourists, including Nelson's Column for £6,000, Big Ben for a grand and Buckingham Palace for a £2,000 down payment – but sadly there's no proof for any of this, so the conman may in fact just be a con.

There is, however, no doubt about who is the granddaddy of fraudsters and conmen everywhere, and he too was a Scot. Called **Gregor MacGregor** (1786–1845), a soldier from Glengyle in Stirlingshire, this one invented an entire kingdom in central America and set out to sell it to the world.

Calling it the Principality of Poyais, and claiming personally to own around eight million acres (12,500 square miles) as its *cazique* or prince, MacGregor proposed leasing smallholdings to investors and colonists for just over three shillings (15p) an acre. The defeat of Napoleon had left Brits feeling buoyant and the French dejected, and by 1822 would-be settlers began setting sail from Leith and from ports in France in search of a new life. At the same time poor returns from British government consuls made Latin American investments look inviting, and money began to pour in to the coffers as MacGregor talked up his imaginary country with details of its great natural wealth and abundant resources. Telling anyone who would listen that the natives were friendly and hardworking, the soil so fertile that three harvests a year were possible, and the country's clear streams almost choked with gold, MacGregor had worked up a sales patter that seemed to be just what everyone wanted to hear. He was also adept at buttering up likely candidates, flattering Highlanders into thinking they had the right spirit and virtues to make the most of this fabulous opportunity, and investors that only they were courageous enough to reap the benefits.

With plans to fill seven ships with settlers, things began to unravel when the first two vessels arrived in the Americas to find – nothing. Back in Europe MacGregor also seemed to be losing it, and while claiming descent from an Inca princess he spent a worrying amount of time devising a new flag for the territory, along with ornate military uniforms and a highly complex honours system. With hindsight perhaps the best to be said is that he was forgetting he had made the whole thing up.

Eventually the French became suspicious, and as more of their people began applying for passports to a country shown on nobody's maps but MacGregor's, the self-styled Inca of New Granada was arrested and found himself in the dock. Inexplicably he was acquitted, despite a paper trail showing a very clear attempt to swindle more than a million pounds at 19th-century prices. Even then he refused to admit defeat, and after remodelling his country to become a republic he emigrated to Venezuela, where in his late fifties he died.

The Worst Reasons for Dialing 999

Presumably in a bid to stop people behaving like idiots, Police Scotland have published details of the stupidest 999 calls recently received:

One thirsty caller contacted the emergency services to find out where he could buy some milk.

Another wanted to complain about a famous fast-food chain, which had served him with a hamburger when a cheeseburger had been ordered.

Sort of on the right track, one late-night caller dialled the emergency number to ask what the non-emergency number was.

A woman was reported for taking illegal drugs that the caller admitted to having bought.

Another rang to ask whether the police (in Scotland) could send someone to an address in Tottenham (in north London) to 'see if my friend is having an affair'.

A man called to report that the telephone he was using had been stolen, another that a neighbour had possibly stolen a beach towel, and a third that there was a pigeon in the garden with a broken wing.

LOST IN LOST

Visitors to Lost in Aberdeenshire frequently lose their way, apparently because other visitors steal the distinctive signs welcoming tourists to the village in Upper Donside. These have proved so popular over the years that the county council formally proposed a name change (to Lost Farm) in a bid to save the more than £100 that each replacement costs. The villagers weren't having any of it, however, and since 2004 the signs have been welded in place in a bid to stop them disappearing. (The author, for his part, has always fancied one of those ones that you see on the A87 in Glen Shiel en route to Sgùrr an t-Searraich, warning, 'FERAL GOATS 2 MILES'.)

17

Gruesome Scotland

'Margaret Wod to be putt to the tortour of the bootes, the
morne, at ten of the clocke, in the Laich Counsell House of
Edinburgh; and that the whole counsell be present when
the tortour is given.'

Orders to the Privy Council, 1 February 1631

Given the brutality and zeal with which Scots have hunted down
witches over the years (see Witchy Scotland, above), it's perhaps
no surprise that authorities in Scotland have also shown a marked
tendency throughout history to use torture rather more than
their counterparts in England and Wales.

Besides resorting to it more often than the neighbours during
the 16th and 17th centuries, Scotland continued to permit the use
of torture long after it had been outlawed south of the border.
With both the king and the Privy Council able to order its use

until as late as 1708, one can only marvel at the cruel and unusual ingenuity of some of the devices employed – particularly because (then as now) simple sleep deprivation was known to be just as effective.

Claiming to have found it in Russia, it was a Scot who returned home with a set of **pilniewinkies** and introduced the native population to the device we know today as the thumbscrew. In reality no more than a crude, portable vice, this was used to crush fingers, thumbs and occasionally toes with such force that the victim's arms would sometimes swell up all the way to the shoulders.

Another simple but brutal persuader was the process known as **thawing**. This involved binding the victim's head with rope as tightly as possible, and then viciously jerking it in different directions repeatedly and with great force.

The medieval **buskin** was a piece of stitched rawhide. After being soaked in water, this would be drawn over the foot and lower leg, and then bound in place with cords. Allowed to dry, or more commonly heated over a slow fire, the garment contracted drastically as the hide dried out. In the process the leg and foot would be squeezed with sufficient force to dislocate the ankle if not actually to shatter the bones.

A more sophisticated version of this was the misleadingly named **Spanish boot**. Constructed using shaped plates of wood or metal, and occasionally fixed to the floor, the device would have the victim's leg inserted into it before wooden wedges were driven in, causing permanent damage to both flesh and bones.

The **caschielawis** was also roughly boot-shaped, and could also be filled with boiling water or even lead (with predictably horrific results), or slowly heated using a portable furnace. In 1594 Thomas Palpa was subjected to a spell in this infernal machine for 'ellewin days and ellewin nychtis', suffering the additional indignity of being 'naikit'. When this didn't work he was then scourged with 'ropes in sic soirt that they left nather flesch nor hyde vpoun him' – until, eventually, he confessed.

Rarely less effective, a prisoner subjected to the **brodequins** would have his or her legs trapped between two tightly bound boards. Again wedges would be driven in – four ordinarily, but eight if 'extraordinary torture' was called for – causing splintering of the bones until, as noted by one unfortunate enough as to observe the process, 'not being able to bear the pain [the accused] promises confession to get rid of it'.

Often used as form of execution as well as torture, the **wheel** was a large wooden structure to which the accused would be attached before his limbs were broken by heavy bludgeoning. In 1603 a servant called John Weir was broken in this manner in Edinburgh, his arms and legs smashed by being repeatedly hit with a heavy agricultural implement. Weir had been found guilty of the murder of a local laird, apparently on the orders of the laird's wife, who was in turn beheaded for her part in the conspiracy.

WELL AND TRULY HOIST

James Douglas, 4th Earl of Morton (1516–81), enjoyed a life of contrasts. He ruled Scotland as regent during the minority of James VI – successfully too, bringing to an end the long civil war with the supporters of Mary, Queen of Scots – but then fell foul of another maiden, the **Maiden**. This was the name given to a primitive kind of guillotine, an example of which can be seen in the National Museum of Scotland, and it has long been held that it was Douglas himself who introduced the first one to Scotland.

Impressed by its 'clean work' after observing an ingenious beheading device known as the Halifax Gibbet (from the Middle English *gibet*, meaning gallows), Douglas is thought to have travelled back across the border with a rough model of the machine. This was then constructed to the right scale by a furniture maker in Edinburgh New

Town, its 75 lb-weighted blade subsequently being used to execute 150 people, before the practice was discontinued in 1716 after the murderer John Hamilton had become its final victim. That Douglas died this way is beyond doubt – his head was to spend eighteen months on a spike outside the High Kirk – but his involvement in its creation is widely believed though not yet proven.

More a punishment than a torture, **whipping at the cart's tail** was a process that involved tying the wrists of the accused to the back of a cart. This would then be led through town while the person being punished, male or female and invariably stripped to the waist, would be lashed repeatedly with a whip of knotted cord. Frequently the courts ordered the ordeal to last until the blood ran freely, and the last person to suffer the punishment was a Glasgow rioter in 1822.

Scotland was also the last place in Britain to order a woman to be **flogged,** an Inverness resident being sentenced to be punished in this way after she was caught being drunk and disorderly in 1817. The practice was halted shortly afterwards but remained on the statute books for men until 1938. Even then it was abolished only because of the public outcry that attended the news that a band of jewel thieves had been subjected to a judicially approved thrashing with a cat-o'-nine-tails.

The last **public hanging** in Scotland took place in Buccleuch Street, Dumfries in 1868, the same town that six years earlier had witnessed the last public execution of a woman. Such events were commonly the cause of great celebration – not least on the part of tavern owners who sold bumper amounts despite boosting prices for the day – but when Jane Timney faced the death penalty for murdering a neighbour, 3,000 women signed a petition to prevent the sentence being carried out.

The local *Kirkcudbrightshire Advertiser* reported that 'the great majority of the public of Dumfries are horrified and indignant that this butchery should be permitted in their streets' but, despite fears of the 'brutalising tendency' of such 'legalised stranglings', the hanging went ahead nevertheless.

SCOTLAND'S LAST EXECUTION

Although a set of gallows was kept in full working order at HMP Wandsworth in London until at least 1994 (and serviced twice a year, as the death penalty was theoretically still available in cases of treason or piracy with violence), the last executions took place some three decades earlier.

In Scotland the very last to suffer the ultimate penalty was 21-year-old Henry John Burnett in August 1963. He was hanged at Craiginches Prison, Aberdeen, after being found guilty of the murder of his girlfriend's husband, a merchant seaman whom he had shot. (The last woman was Susan Newall at Glasgow's Duke Street Prison in 1923. She strangled a paperboy – possibly to get his money – and then attempted to frame her husband for the crime.)

In 1969 capital punishment was finally abolished for murders of this kind, but in 2009 a survey by Channel Four suggested that more than half of Scots (55% as opposed to 49% of English respondents) would like to see it made available to the courts once again. Nearly three-quarters also said they would like to see a return to the death penalty for other crimes including armed robbery, rape, terrorism, treason, child abuse and kidnapping.

Minnie Dean and the Missing Children

In 1895 Greenock-born Williamina 'Minnie' Dean became the only woman ever to be hanged on the instructions of a New Zealand court. The daughter of a railway engineer, Dean had emigrated several years previously, and after posing as a doctor's widow she set herself up as a so-called baby farmer. The job entailed taking young children in for money, and was common enough in Victorian times, when an absence of effective contraception and a fear of scandal led many single mothers to conceal unwanted children.

Dean was by no means unusual in preferring the money to the babies, and in England around the same time Amelia Dyer is thought to have murdered as many as 400 small children. Dean escaped detection for years, not least because the odd death rarely looked suspicious in an era when infant mortality was so high. In 1895, however, she was spotted boarding a train with a baby and a hatbox, and then leaving without the baby. A search of her backyard uncovered three corpses including the baby (which had been strangled), another that had been drugged, and a third for which no cause of death could be positively identified.

Whilst maintaining her innocence and insisting all three children had died of natural causes, Dean was nevertheless unable to account for a total of fourteen of the twenty-eight children who had been entrusted to her care. Accordingly, on 12 August 1895 the Scotswoman was hanged by New Zealand executioner Tom Long (no relation) on gallows erected at the intersection of two Scottish-sounding streets, Spey and Leven, in the decidedly Scottish sounding city of Invercargill.

Grave Robbing: A Public Service

Whilst Burke and Hare certainly took things to an altogether different level (see below), grave-robbing already had a long history in Scotland, and resurrection men working in the big cities never wanted for customers. A major part of the problem was a refusal on the part of the authorities fully to acknowledge just how many bodies were needed for dissection. Since 1505 the law allowed the surgeons of Edinburgh access to just one corpse a year to share between all of them, typically that of a murderer cut down from the scaffold. Their counterparts in London fared little better – they were allowed only four – and with the medical profession growing at a pace it was simply not sufficient.

Even when a new law was introduced in 1752 so that a majority of murderers would be hanged and then dissected, the change was made not to alleviate the problem but merely to provide an even harsher penalty in the hope that the murder rate would be forced down. It failed on both counts, and with bodies still in short supply, and up to a thousand medical students in each city desperate to learn more about man's inner workings, medical schools in London and Edinburgh knew where to turn for more.

Incredibly, stealing a corpse was not a serious crime in the 18th century – it was considered far less serious, for example, than stealing the coffin, which, unlike a corpse, was regarded in law as someone's property. Admittedly, the crime seriously offended the public's sense of decency, but for decades the courts continued to regard the trade of the bodysnatcher as no more than a misdemeanour, providing those in the dock had remembered to steal only the body and not the shroud or coffin.

Perhaps because of this lenient approach, medical students often took things into their own hands. So too did the public, and in 1813 in Glasgow a furious mob broke into the home of the university's Professor of Anatomy when a number of students had given them the slip after being seen ransacking the grave of a recently deceased woman in the churchyard at Ramshorn. As events threatened to get out of hand the police were called. They found female body parts concealed around the house, and arrested those inside. Charges were laid against four individuals, including the professor, but, incredibly, all four got off. The prosecution was unable to prove that the body parts they had hidden belonged to the missing woman. No one doubted they were human, but neither could anyone prove where they had come from.

With so little risk accompanying what was fast becoming a relatively lucrative crime, it soon fell to organised gangs to secure the cadavers. Some imported corpses from Ireland, where they could be had for as little as 10/- (50p), although one imagines that the logistics of delivery meant the quality suffered. Others took genuine pride in their work and – unlike the students, who tended just to smash and grab – would expertly lever off the end of a coffin and remove the body head first. In this way, by disturbing the grave as little as possible, the best of them were thus able to return to the same burial grounds more than once.

It was perhaps that same professional pride which resulted in at least one gang member remonstrating with magistrates when he was eventually hauled into court. Wouldn't their worships be better employed locking up thieves and scoundrels, he asked, than in 'apprehending respectable men who lived by supplying the Faculty with subjects for dissection?'

His defence depended on him claiming to provide a public service, which in a sense he did as an informal or freelance agent for the advancement of science. But the public despised such creatures, and once the activities of Burke and Hare had come to light – as we shall see, it demonstrated how a shortage of subjects for dissection could provide a perfect incentive for mass murder – the authorities had to move. In 1832 a new Anatomy Act outlawed the use of executed criminals in this way, and provided a legitimate route through which unclaimed bodies could pass from hospital ward and parish workhouse to the medical school slab.

Burke and Hare ... and McDougal and Laird

Whilst frequently remembered as mere bodysnatchers – as if that crime were not bad enough – William Burke and William Hare were actually serial killers, a pair of Irish labourers who in pretty short order were responsible for killing sixteen victims and selling their bodies to a corrupt Edinburgh surgeon.

Each body yielded a profit of between £7 and £10, the grisly entrepreneurs apparently finding murder preferable to (and perhaps more pleasurable than) the backbreaking work of actually digging up the dead. They had useful accomplices, too – in Burke's girlfriend Helen McDougal and Margaret Laird, Hare's wife – and a ready market for their wares in a world where cadavers were in short supply for students wishing to advance their skills at Surgeon's Square

The victims were all local to Tanner's Close where the pair lodged, the first in 1827 a tenant who died owing rent, which they cleverly decided to recoup by selling his body. Thereafter they took to suffocating their victims, a method still known as 'burking', which left the body in a fit state to be anatomised. Unsurprisingly, they preferred those who were feeble in mind or body, a dozen of whom were female, and several of them drunks.

When their crimes came to light Burke confessed, both to the authorities and at length in an edition of the *Edinburgh Evening Courant*. His fate thus sealed, he was hanged in Lawnmarket on the morning of 28 January 1829. Despite appalling weather, a crowd of 25,000 thronged the surrounding streets, some of the better-off paying a pound for a good vantage point overlooking the scaffold. Hare, however, escaped punishment, having turned king's evidence and testified against his erstwhile friend. To the disgust of the crowd, so too did the two women, although they were later stoned and run out of town.

Hare's eventual fate is still unknown, but Burke never left Edinburgh again and after being flayed and publicly dissected his skeleton was put on display at Surgeon's Square. Today it lives under lock and key at Edinburgh University – in order, as the judge told him, 'that posterity may keep in remembrance of your atrocious crimes' – together with a book and a small box bound in pieces of his skin.

18

Screening Scotland

'I'm an actor. It's not brain surgery. If I do my job right, people won't ask for their money back.'

Sean Connery

A Baird Influence?

Television made something of a late start in Scotland, surprisingly so as the thing was invented by one high-profile Scot while another one ran the first broadcaster.

With its famous motto over the front door – 'Nation Shall Speak Unto Nation', adapted from a line in the Old Testament – Lord Reith's BBC was so small to begin with that during the 1926 General Strike it broadcast from his study at home. But even when it grew large enough and powerful enough to move into its present home, Broadcasting House, it remained for a long time a London-based organisation.

It took until the 1950s before Scots could pick up the signal from that far south, and not everyone welcomed the intrusion. The rector of Aberdeen University described television as an even greater menace than radio, 'a tangible terror' that was about to insinuate itself into the lives of ordinary people; others worried that it would divert children from their homework. Though Reith was a Kincardineshire man (born in Stonehaven) there were also the inevitable concerns about undue English influence, particularly at a time when nearly two million Scots had signed the Scottish Covenant, a petition calling for an independent Edinburgh Parliament.

In fact, initially at least, they needn't have worried: to begin with Scotland had just a single transmitter, at Kirk O'Shotts on a barren moor in Lanarkshire. This only worked providing the mast rigger managed to scale it once a week to chip off the huge lumps of ice that formed around the summit. It also relied on a signal that travelled underground from London to the Pennines and then via a series of seven smaller masts and a reflecting dish on the ramparts of Edinburgh Castle. Even later, when additional transmitters were installed, there were many problems, such as Perth viewers getting sound only, and those in Orkney being treated to what the local *Herald* newspaper called 'a fluorescent blizzard'.

But, unsurprisingly, once regular broadcasts began in March 1952 the public loved it, although even then it took well over a decade before viewing figures in Scotland rivalled the number of radio listeners. Part of the problem was that most Scots just couldn't afford a television of their own: a tax introduced in the 1951 budget had raised the price of even the cheapest set to around £60 (equivalent to around £1,200 today).

Fortunately, most didn't mind sharing the experience. In Glasgow thousands queued to watch a set installed at Parkhead

Public Hall, 300 at a time being allowed in for each strictly measured half-hour shift, and outside Mallaig viewers trooped out in the night to see a battery-powered set that had been positioned on a hill to catch the signal.

On 31 August 1957 the BBC found itself with a competitor, in the shape of the new, independent Scottish Television. This broadcast from Glasgow's Theatre Royal, although it was majority-owned by a Canadian businessman who employed a fellow Canadian as his station head.Programme quality was often very poor to begin with, but particularly in remote areas viewers were keen not to miss out, and began to show the kind of entrepreneurial spirit for which Scots are famous. For example, by the time the authorities officially hooked up the Outer Hebrides (via a mast on Wester Ross in 1965), several thousand islanders had already been enjoying television courtesy of a second-hand mast that had been acquired independently for £25. On Harris, the famous tweed weavers were also delighted to find that their more sophisticated new looms could be operated while watching television. The loom would automatically stop if a thread snapped or got snagged whether the weaver was paying attention or watching the box.

Even so, and well into the 1960s, Scottish churchmen and women were still railing against the 'flood of lurid salacious material' pouring into homes, the Synod of Glenelg in Lochalsh observing sadly that 'the Sabbath, for some unknown reason, seems to be the day when the medium excels in its foul moral oozings'.

They might have liked the idea of Gaelic television, however, which has the great advantage that almost nobody can understand it. By 1981 something under 2% of Scots spoke Gaelic, and of this total (82,000, according to the official census) it seems reasonable to suppose that all of them spoke fluent Scots-English as well. Nationalist-minded broadcasters still had a long-held desire for a distinctively Scottish channel, however, and saw their chance with the passing of the 1990 Broadcasting Act.

The Act called for Gaelic programming, and more significantly provided a budget for it. A decision was therefore taken to provide Scottish viewers with programmes the vast majority of them neither wanted nor could understand, and under the BBC Alba banner the initiative continues to this day. Its supporters insist it will grow the number of Gaelic speakers, but so far there is no sign of this happening. By the time of the 2011 Census the total had dipped to well below 60,000, which if nothing else must go some way to explaining the station's decision to include English subtitles.

Scotland in the Movies

The 39 Steps (1935)

With the British film industry desperate to break into international markets, Alfred Hitchcock's only Scottish film was enormously expensive for the time, its budget of £60,000 being at least 50% greater than his previous one, *The Man Who Knew Too Much*. Preferable to the remakes, it is frequently voted a favourite by film buffs who don't seem to mind that, having crossed the Forth Bridge, the hero, Richard Hannay, finds himself immediately in the Highlands around Glen Coe and Rannoch Moor.

Whisky Galore (1949)

This fact-based if fanciful Ealing comedy tells the story of the plundered cargo of thousands of cases of whisky that were looted from the SS *Politician* after she ran aground off Eriskay in 1941. Bottles from the ship still occasionally wash up and fetch huge sums, but an estimated 75,000 10/- notes have never been accounted for, although these were known to have been carried on board. The film itself was largely shot on Barra (with locals earning £1 as extras), and it had to be renamed *Tight Little Island* in the US, where there was a ban on films with alcohol in the titles.

2001: A Space Odyssey (1968)

This is not generally regarded as a Scottish film, but one of the more curious aspects of its production was director Stanley Kubrick's decision to utilise the peaty moorland of the island of Harris and various rock clusters situated on its eastern coastline to simulate the surface of Jupiter for a fly-over scene.

The Prime of Miss Jean Brodie (1969)

Because the 'gels' were played by adults – at least one of whom had children of her own – the desks were raised up in order to make them look smaller. (The actresses were also asked not to wear school uniforms in the Pinewood canteen as this served alcohol.) When the film was shown as a Royal Command Performance the art class scene was cut because a drawing of a male nude is briefly shown. This is especially bizarre as consideration was given to showing *Sweet Charity* instead, a film based on a Federico Fellini screenplay about a prostitute.

The Wicker Man (1974)

Created as a vehicle for Christopher Lee, this cult horror flick also stars Britt Ekland, much of whose part was dubbed. (The famous scene in which she dances naked was similarly shot largely using a body double.) For more than forty years the remains of the Wicker Man could still be seen near a campsite in Galloway – other scenes were filmed at Plockton, on Skye and in Ayrshire – but in 2006 the two wooden stumps were stolen and have never been recovered.

Gregory's Girl (1981)

Bill Forsyth's engaging coming-of-age comedy was set in a school in Abronhill in Cumbernauld and made with a budget of just £200,000 by using students from Glasgow's Youth Theatre. Most wore their own clothes, while one of the female leads, Dee Hepburn, was sent off for a few weeks' training at Partick Thistle FC, as her role required some skill at soccer. Starring opposite her, the singer Clare Grogan had to be filmed mostly in profile as she had been severely injured by flying glass after witnessing a fight at Glasgow's Pollock Inn.

Local Hero (1983)

Forsyth's next film is sometimes likened to *Whisky Galore* in that it pitches wily villagers against big business in the shape of Burt Lancaster's Texas oilman, Felix Happer. Fans of the film arriving at Pennan in Aberdeenshire, the model for 'Ferness' in the film, face disappointment, however, as the beach scenes were filmed many miles away at Morar, Camusdarach, Moidart and Arisaig on the west coast. The telephone box is also slightly bogus, having been installed to replace the prop one that was used to such good effect in the film. However, in a charming coda, the billionaire Texan's quest to find a comet in the skies over Scotland was finally realised in 1992, when a newly discovered asteroid was officially named '7345 Happer'.

Highlander (1986)

Originally contracted to write just one song of the film, the members of Queen reportedly enjoyed seeing early rushes so much that they agreed to do the whole soundtrack. Extras arriving for the fight scene set at Eilean Donan were promised an extra £10 a day if they brought their own horses, and the fighter jet seen at the end was supplied by RAF Lossiemouth. The film's star Christophe Lambert had an earlier connection with Scotland – *Greystoke* was filmed in part at the Duke of Roxburghe's Floors Castle – although with only two lines to speak as Tarzan in that one his heavily accented English was less of a concern.

Soft Top, Hard Shoulder (1993)

Written by and starring Peter Capaldi, this unlikely Strathclyde-set road movie sees the future *Dr Who* protagonist as the scion of a Glaswegian-Italian ice-cream dynasty piloting a decrepit Triumph Herald in a bid not to miss his father's sixtieth birthday. Along the way he picks up an annoying hitch-hiker played by his real-life wife, Elaine Collins.

Shallow Grave (1994)

With a nod to the *Wicker Man* – at one point Ewan MacGregor's character is seen watching the film – this low-budget black comedy focuses on three Edinburgh flatmates struggling to conceal the body of a fourth (played by Lily Allen's dad, Keith). It was shot mostly in Glasgow as the city came up with £150,000, and despite taking just four weeks to film it was the year's most successful British movie.

Trainspotting (1996)

Keith Allen returns, again as a drug dealer, in the decade-defining film of Irvine Welsh's novel. For a while Danny Boyle considered subtitles in order to make the characters intelligible to an American audience, but in the end it was agreed simply to re-record the opening scenes with the actors softening their accents to sound a bit less Scottish. Also: the faeces in the loo were apparently made from chocolate, although knowing this may not help.

MOVIES ON THE MOVE

An industrial warehouse, a Gothic gallery, the world-famous Kelvingrove Museum and the hold of a tall ship were just some of the unusual pop-up venues showing movies at the tenth annual Glasgow Film Festival in 2014, but perhaps none could hold a candle to the so-called Screen Machine. This eighty-seat, air-conditioned mobile cinema has been bringing the latest films to remote and rural areas of Scotland for more than fifteen years. Visiting thirty or so isolated communities in the Highlands and Western Isles on an annual tour lasting approximately ten weeks, it is the only cinema in the United Kingdom to require an MOT certificate.

Mrs Brown (1997)

The story of Queen Victoria's highland fling was originally made for television, but made it into cinemas apparently because impresario Harvey Weinstein liked it so much. Judi Dench plays the queen, and her real-life niece Finty Williams her on-screen daughter. (Confusingly, the actresses playing her ladies-in-waiting are also the same ones who play Queen Elizabeth's in *Shakespeare in Love*.) Filming took place in Duns Castle in the Borders and at various locations on the Ardverikie Estate in Badenoch. During his time on set Paisley-born actor Gerard Butler received an award after pulling a struggling swimmer from the Tay, but then caught hypothermia after running naked into a lake with Billy Connolly.

Sweet Sixteen (2002)

Ken Loach's tough but tender Greenock tale caused controversy at the time, receiving an '18' certificate as a result of the high incidence of swear words. The one beginning with F was used 313 times and the even worse one twenty times, but the makers objected on the grounds that such language was more common up north (and so less offensive). The authorities held firm, except in Inverclyde where it was allowed to slip through as a '15'. Elsewhere subtitles were provided to assist non-Scots.

The Illusionist (2010)

When a French illusionist finds himself out of work and travels to Scotland, cinemagoers were treated to several subtle digs at the political situation of the time. A passing car has the registration FU2 BUSH, and a pawnbroker clearly modelled on an Edinburgh establishment is called Blair & Brown. The leading character is also seen entering a restaurant, McDaunnalds, on Victoria Street. (Readers should also note that the film is based on a script of Jacques Tati's that is set in the Czech Republic, but it should not be confused with the 2006 film also called *The Illusionist* that was merely filmed there.)

Neds (2010)

A ned or non-educated delinquent, being a Glaswegian yob or hooligan, the film explores 1970s gang culture in the city using a gritty mix of English and local dialect. The award-winning script was written and directed by Peter Mullan (previously seen in *Shallow Grave*, *Trainspotting* and *Braveheart*), who makes an appearance as part of an excellent but largely unknown cast of youngsters.

OCH, HOOTS, MON

With the possible exception of Sean Connery's Scottish-Russian in *Hunt for Red October*, or his Spanish-Egyptian

---

in *Highlander*, it's likely no one will ever plumb the depths of bad-accentry Dick Van Dyke explored with his woeful cockernee in *Mary Poppins*. Crimes against the Scottish accent continue to be perpetrated, however, with the following most often cited as the worst offenders:

Frenchman **Christophe Lambert** apparently learned to speak English only very shortly before joining Connery to star in *Highlander* (1986). He was given a dialogue coach to help out, but more than twenty years after the film's release his was still being voted the worst Scottish accent of all time, and the result likened by one critic to the performance of a drunken Norwegian.

Canadian **Mike Myers** is known to have a thing about Scotland, but that hardly explains the liberties he took with the tongue in the second *Austin Powers* movie and throughout the whole of the box office-busting *Shrek* series. At best he sounds a bit like Ewan McGregor, but he's never as good as Ewan McGregor and not like him often to excuse the rest.

Another Canadian to get it all horribly wrong is *Star Trek's* **James Doohan.** For years he played the Chief Engineer of the *Enterprise*, a character helpfully called 'Scotty' Scot in case viewers cannae tell from his accent that he's meant to be from Linlithgow. (Subsequent reiterations of the show have seen **Simon Pegg** offer up a bad Scottish accent of his own, but whether in error or homage it is hard to tell.)

Knowing they can get by sounding like themselves, a few really big stars seem almost to trade on it by not bothering to change. Listening to **Michael Caine** in *Kidnapped* (1971) it's a pity he didn't stick to his normal 'sahf Lahndahn' instead of making an effort to fit in.

Most of the cast of *Rob Roy* (1995) could pass for

Scottish, but not **Jessica Lange**, whose lavishly rolling R at times threatens to tip over into parody.

The flaws in *Braveheart* (1995) are so numerous it seems churlish to pick out **Mel Gibson**'s accent, but if you're going to rewrite history you don't have to mangle the narrative as well by switching between Aussie, American and sort-of-Scots each time the scene changes.

Fortunately it's only an advertisement for Dewar's Whisky, which given time we shall all forget, but the cod-Scots accent dished up in 2013 by Anglo-Italian **Claire Forlani** is definitely inexcusable for someone married to a Scotsman (Dougray Scott, from Glenrothes).

It's a toss-up as to which is the least convincing – **Robert Duvall**'s accent or Ally McCoist's acting – but for some reason *A Shot at Glory* (2001), about a small-time football team, didn't play well at the box office or with reviewers.

As the divorced hero of *Mrs Doubtfire* (1993), **Robin Williams** dons a dress to disguise himself and so maintain contact with his children. Unfortunately his attempt at a Scottish accent is so lame that a joke about how lame it is seems to have been inserted into the script simply to get the actor and/or director off the hook.

Isla Fisher has taken a pasting for her iffy Scottish accent in *Burke and Hare* (2010). In her defence it could be said that she's Australian, but then her parents are from Bathgate and Stranraer, and she's married to Sacha Baron Cohen, who seems capable of nailing just about every accent on the planet.

19

Consuming Scotland

'My theory is that all of Scottish cuisine is based on a dare.'

Mike Myers

It's Not All Deep-fried Mars Bars (But Do Try One)

In his celebrated dictionary Samuel Johnson memorably defined oats as 'a grain, which in England is generally given to horses, but in Scotland supports the people', but then was honest enough to admit in his *Journey to the Western Islands of Scotland* that, 'if an epicure could remove by a wish, in quest of sensual gratifications, wherever he had supped he would breakfast in Scotland'. It's fair to say that Scottish cuisine has never enjoyed the highest reputation – not helped by Scotland being the second fattest country in the developed world – but fair to say too, perhaps, that it has never quite enjoyed the reputation it probably deserves . . .

A Scottish classic of flour, sugar, and butter, **shortbread** is popularly supposed to have been invented by Mary, Queen of Scots, but almost certainly derives from hard, medieval biscuit-bread of a sort commonly consumed in the 12th century. Initially expensive, rejigged as shortbread, it was for years reserved for special occasions such as birthdays and Hogmanay, and decorated shortbread cakes or *bonns* are traditionally still broken over the heads of Shetland brides.

Lancashire makes a dangerous claim for the world's first 'hagese', but as **haggis** Scotland's delicious national dish made its debut appearance in a poem around 1510 ('*Schir Johine the Ros*', or 'The Flyting of Dunbar and Kennedie'). Today the sheep's stomach lining is commonly replaced by conventional sausage casing, but this modification has not been enough to persuade those for whom a mix of onion, oatmeal, suet, spices and 'pluck' (heart, lung and liver) sounds too grim to bear.

IS HAGGIS UNHOLY

Following their introduction to Europe in the 16th century, **potatoes** were briefly fashionable and wildly popular. In France Louis XVI of France wore a potato flower in his buttonhole and Marie Antoinette a spray in her hair, and in Spain they were considered so exotic that people assumed they were a species of truffle. Scots were very slow to acquire the habit of eating them, however, with many refusing even to consider them as they aren't mentioned in the Bible. But then last time someone looked neither was haggis.

Despite a similarity to Indian *khichri*, and its decidedly un-Scottish moniker, **kedgeree**, maintains the National Trust for

Scotland, originated here around 1790. The Trust insists the recipe travelled to the Raj with soldiers of the Scottish regiments before being reborn as the popular haddock-based Anglo-Indian breakfast dish and brought back to the British Isles.

Henry VIII is known to have received a gift of a 'box of marmalade' from a Devon man more than 250 years earlier, but Scotland produced the first **commercial marmalade brand** in Dundee in 1797. Whilst it is almost certainly not true that Janet Keiller devised the recipe after her husband acquired a ship's cargo of storm-damaged oranges from Seville, the inclusion of rind may have been her idea. James Keiller and Son, trading since 1828, is also thought to have created the first **Dundee cake.**

By far the most popular Indian food in Britain, but famously one never found on the sub-continent, **chicken tikka masala** is thought to have originated in Gibson Street, Glasgow, where chef Ali Ahmed Aslam improvised a new sauce of yogurt, tomato soup, cream and spices. Admittedly, a rival claim is made for a restaurant somewhere in north London, but at the time of writing there is talk of the Glasgow authorities seeking to have some kind of official EU-protected designation of origin status granted for the enduring Asian dish.

NOT SO WEE DRAM: THE WORLD'S MOST
EXPENSIVE WHISKIES*

£7,500	Macallan 55-Year-Old Lalique Crystal Decanter
£10,000	Glenfiddich 50-Year-Old
£11,000	Highland Park 50-Year-Old Single Malt
£36,000	Dalmore 62 Single Hiland Malt Scotch
£46,000	1926 Macallan Fine and Rare Collection
£100,000	Dalmore 64 Trinitas
£125,000	62-Year-Old Dalmore
£290,000	64-Year-Old Macallan

£875,000   105-Year-Old Master of Malt
£3,875,000 Isabella's Islay

*Prices are approximate, and as a fool and his money are
so readily parted (particularly when alcohol is involved),
almost certainly out of date by the time you read this. Note
too that the price includes the bottle, an important consideration when, for example, the last named is delivered
in a bespoke English crystal decanter studded with 8,500
diamonds, 300 rubies and some tidy white gold detailing.

Dating back to 1995, that first **deep-fried Mars bar** was sold in
Stonehaven, at the Haven Fish Bar. Almost certainly intended as
a novelty item, as supposed 'proof' of Scotland's reputation for
producing and enjoying the world's least healthy cuisine, it was
assured of massive media coverage and cult status quickly followed
the tabloid headlines. The craze for the things duly caught on,
despite a spokesman from the Mars Corporation insisting that the
practice ran foul of his company's commitment to healthy eating.

The bestselling soft drink in Scotland, **Irn-Bru** may no longer
be made from girders but it still contains 0.002% of ammonium
ferric citrate among its more than thirty different flavouring
agents. It was first produced in Falkirk more than a century ago,
and is still made by an independent company, A.G. Barr.

You'll also find a Scotsman behind the best-selling **Japanese
lager**. The Kirin Brewing Company, Japan's largest, was founded
by a Scottish merchant. Thomas Blake Glover left Aberdeenshire
for the Far East in 1859, initially to buy green tea, and the mous-
tache on the 'kirin', a mythical creature depicted on the label, is
said to be based on his splendidly traditional Victorian whiskers.

While the world continues to argue about which country
invented whisky, Scotland can lay claim to the rival **gin and tonic**.

It was an Edinburgh-born physician and Army surgeon, George Cleghorn (1716–94), who suggested quinine as a preventative for the malaria that was afflicting so many servants of the Empire. Apparently when dissolved in tonic the quinine bark extract was so bitter that the gin had to be added, if only to flavour the pill.

Lime cordial has similarly medicinal origins, and was first bottled and sold by Lachlan Rose, the son of a Leith shipbuilder, who saw it as a sensible ocean-going cure for scurvy in the days of sail. Funnily enough, this also mixes astonishing well with gin, as generations of Royal Navy officers will attest.

No such claims are made for the **world's strongest beer** but this too is Scottish, and comes from the small town of Keith, where Banffshire's Brewmeister Brewery produces something called Snake Venom. Boasting an astonishing 67.5% rating for alcohol-by-volume, the brewery says it was created in response to complaints that at only 65% its existing Armageddon brew was simply too weak. Created over nine months by partners Lewis Shand and John Mackenzie using smoked pea malt and two different yeasts, it costs £50 for a small 275ml bottle and is presumably not intended to be drunk in pints.

Scotland's **first fish and chips** arrived courtesy of migrants from northern Italy, who were selling *pesce e patata* in this country from the 1890s onwards. Thirty years earlier, according to the National Federation of Fish Friers, the dish had been invented by Joseph Malin, an east London Jew who first combined traditional Jewish fried fish with the newly fashionable chipped potato. But north of the border the Italians established a firm hold, and by 1914 they completely dominated the market with shops and take-away restaurants across much of Scotland.

ICE CREAM, CHOLERA AND PROSTITUTION

The Italians were of course also largely responsible for introducing **ice cream** to the UK, a treat that proved so especially popular in Scotland that by 1905 there were already more than 300 Italian-owned ice-cream parlours in Glasgow alone. Indeed, it was the turf wars between various vendors that led many to leave the trade altogether and switch to selling *pesce e patate*.

But not everyone welcomed the Italians' arrival. Long before the fighting broke out, the medical journal *The Lancet* had attributed various cholera outbreaks to what it referred to as poisonous Italian ice-cream. In particular, they blamed the way it was served, describing grubby glasses that were quickly rinsed in filthy water containing 'mouth secretions of previous buyers', before being 'swabbed with a small wet offensive cloth and up-ended on a soiled barrow top'. (Eventually the cone was invented expressly to alleviate this sort of concern, although a habit among vendors of licking the drips off before handing it to customers almost certainly made things worse.)

There were other concerns too, especially over what might be called the moral dimension. For many there was a suspicion that a liking for ice-cream could prove a slippery slope for any unmarried women who tasted it. In particular the authorities were concerned about what went on in the parlours, chiefly because there were suddenly so many of them, all of them in foreign hands (worse: Roman Catholic hands) and of course they were frequented by the young.

In some quarters of the Scottish establishment there were fears that the frozen dessert couldn't fail to have a subversive effect on consumers, and that after having their first taste of ice cream young girls would move effortlessly on to try cigarettes, and then kissing, and ultimately a career as a prostitute or streetwalker. All this, remember, in places that sold no alcohol but which nevertheless had their opponents warning of the perils of 'luxury being smuggled into

> the souls of Glaswegians', and the Glasgow *Herald* railing against establishments its correspondent affected to find 'ten times worse than any of the evils of the public-house'.

In most countries of the world the word skink describes a large variety of lizard, and one few would wish to eat. In Scotland, however, a **Cullen Skink** is a kind of chowder, a thick soup of potato, onion and smoked haddock originating from the north-eastern town of that name. Curiously, 'skink' here derives from the Gaelic for a beef shinbone (i.e. a shank in English), although these are never used in its preparation.

Said to come from the happiest cattle in Europe, **Isle of Mull Cheddar** is uniquely tangy thanks to the slightly alcoholic milk on which its production relies. The diet of the cows in question includes 'draff', the spent husks of the fermented grain used in the nearby Tobermory whisky distillery. The relatively low proportion of grass consumed by the beasts explains the light, almost ivory hue of the finished cheese.

Could a soup be more Scottish than **cock-a-leekie**? Apparently yes. It's been enjoyed here since the dying days of the 16th century, but the name didn't come into general usage for nearly 200 years, recognising somewhat belatedly that it was a recipe borrowed from the French and with the onions switched for locally grown leeks.

And finally, who can deny that the Scots have the **best ever food joke**? A woman goes into a Glasgow cake shop and asks, 'Is that a doughnut or a meringue?' The shop assistant replies, 'No, you're right. It's a doughnut.'